ROYAL COURT

Royal Court Theatre presents

I JUST STOPPED BY TO SEE THE MAN

by **Stephen Jeffreys**

First performance at the Royal Court Jerwood Theatre Downstairs, Sloane Square, London on 30 November 2000

Recipient of an **AT&T**: _OnStage_ award **AT&T**

Supported by Royal Court Stage Hands

I JUST STOPPED BY TO SEE THE MAN

by **Stephen Jeffreys**

Cast in order of appearance
Karl **Ciarán McMenamin**
Jesse **Tommy Hollis**
Della **Sophie Okonedo**

Director **Richard Wilson**
Designer **Julian McGowan**
Lighting Designer **Johanna Town**
Sound Designer **Paul Arditti**
Assistant Director **Dawn Walton**
Music Advisor **Guy Pratt**
Casting Director **Lisa Makin**
Production Manager **Paul Handley**
Company Stage Manager **Cath Binks**
Stage Management **Pea Horsley, Rachael Claire Lovett, Maxine Foo**
Costume Supervisor **Iona Kenrick, Suzanne Duffy**
Company Voice Work **Patsy Rodenburg**
Dialect Coach **Jeannette Nelson**
Set Construction **Souvenir**

Royal Court Theatre would like to thank the following for their help with this production:
Wardrobe care by Persil and Comfort courtesy of Lever Brothers Ltd.
Tommy Hollis is appearing with the kind permission of Actors' Equity Association pursuant to an exchange programme between British Equity and American Equity with the assistance of American Conservatory Theater, San Francisco.

AT&T: OnStage

AT&T has been a leading corporate sponsor of the arts for almost 60 years, partnering with the world's finest cultural institutions to promote innovation in the visual arts, theater, film, dance, music, and opera.

"The Hunchback of Notre Dame: 1482," an AT&T OnStage production by Robert Rosen, Paul Walsh, and Steve Epp and performed at Théâtre de la Jeune Lune (Minneapolis). Photo Credit: Michal Daniel.

AT&T OnStage is AT&T's international theater program. It was created in 1985 to encourage performing arts organizations to develop and present original new works for the stage, with particular emphasis on the work of women and artists of diverse cultures. Since its inception, AT&T OnStage has sponsored over 60 new productions in the United States, Canada, and the United Kingdom.

The AT&T OnStage production of "Ballad of Yachiyo," by Philip Kan Gotanda, performed at the Berkeley Repertory Theatre and South Coast Repertory (Costa Mesa). Photo Credit: Ken Friedman.

The AT&T OnStage production of August Wilson's "Seven Guitars," which was performed at the Goodman Theatre (Chicago) and subsequently at the Huntington Theater (Boston), the American Conservatory Theatre (San Francisco), the Mark Taper Forum (Los Angeles), and on Broadway. Photo Credit: Eric Y. Exit.

"I Just Stopped by to See the Man," by Stephen Jeffreys is an exciting addition to the 2000 roster of seven new plays sponsored by AT&T OnStage in Honolulu, San Diego, New York, New Brunswick (NJ), and London. AT&T is proud to support "I Just Stopped by to See the Man" and is pleased to be associated with the Royal Court Theatre and the many cultural institutions where innovation and the diverse voices of society are celebrated.

THE COMPANY

Stephen Jeffreys (writer)
For the Royal Court: The Libertine.
Other theatre: A Going Concern, Valued Friends
(Hampstead); The Clink, Returning Fire (Pines
Plough); The Garden of Eden (Pocket Theatre
Cumbria).
Adaptations include: Hard Times (Pocket Theatre
Cumbria), Carmen (performed by Communicado
at the Tricycle), A Jovial Crew (RSC).
Awards include the Evening Standard and Critics'
Circle Awards for Most Promising Playwright for
Valued Friends.

Paul Arditti (sound designer)
Paul Arditti has been designing sound for theatre
since 1983. He currently combines his post as
Head of Sound at the Royal Court (where he has
designed more than 60 productions) with regular
freelance projects.
For the Royal Court: Far Away, The Force of
Change, My Zinc Bed, 4.48 Psychosis, Fireface,
Mr Kolpert, The Force of Change, Hard Fruit,
Other People, Dublin Carol, Breath, Boom, The
Kitchen, Rat in the Skull, Some Voices, Mojo, The
Lights, The Weir; The Steward of Christendom,
Shopping and Fucking, Blue Heart (co-production
with Out of Joint); The Chairs (co production with
Theatre de Complicite); The Strip, Never Land
(co-production with the Foundry), Cleansed,
Via Dolorosa, Real Classy Affair.
Other theatre includes: Light (Complicite); Our
Lady of Sligo (RNT with Out of Joint); Some
Explicit Polaroids (Out of Joint); Hamlet, The
Tempest (RSC); Orpheus Descending, Cyrano de
Bergerac, St Joan (West End); Marathon (Gate).
Musicals includes: Doctor Dolittle, Piaf, The
Threepenny Opera.
Awards include: Drama Desk Award for
Outstanding Sound Design 1992 for Four Baboons
Adoring the Sun (Broadway).

Tommy Hollis
Theatre includes: Ragtime (Ford Center for the
Performing Arts, NYC); Seven Guitars (Walter
Kerr); Showboat (North Shore Music Festival);
Bailey's Café (Hartford Stage); Love, Langston
(Seattle Repertory); Betsy Brown (McCarter
Theatre); Solid Gold Cadillac (Yale Repertory); Lost
in the Stars (Long Wharf Theatre); The Piano
Lesson (Walter Kerr, NYC).
Television includes: Mary and Rhonda, Mama
Flora's Family, Homicide, Law and Order, New
York Undercover, Zooman and the Sign, Queen,
I'll Fly Away, As the World Turns, Stay the Night,
Separate but Equal, Guiding Light.
Film includes: Primary Colors, The Professional,
Vernon John's Story, Malcolm X, Ghostbusters,
Skylight.

Julian McGowan (designer)
For the Royal Court: Mr Kolpert, Toast, The
Censor, American Bagpipes, The Treatment;
The Steward of Christendom, Blue Heart
(with Out of Joint).
Other theatre includes: Four Nights at
Knaresborough (New Vic Workshop at the
Tricycle), Enjoy, Blast From the Past, Tess of
the D'Urbervilles (West Yorkshire Playhouse);
Some Explicit Polaroids (Out of Joint); Waiting
for Godot, Don Juan, The Lodger, Women
Laughing (Royal Exchange, Manchester); Our
Lady of Sligo (Out of Joint/RNT); Our
Country's Good (Out of Joint/Young Vic); The
Positive Hour (Out of Joint/Hampstead);
Shopping and Fucking (Ambassadors/Out of
Joint); The Possibilities, Venice Preserv'd, The
LA Plays (Almeida); Heart Throb (Bush); The
Wives' Excuse (Royal Shakespeare Company);
Caesar and Cleopatra, Total Eclipse, A Tale of
Two Cities (Greenwich); The Rivals, Man and
Superman, Playboy of the Western World,
Hedda Gabler.
Opera includes: Cosi Fan Tutte (New Israeli
Opera); Eugene Onegin (Scottish Opera);
Siren Song (Almeida Opera Festival).

Ciarán McMenamin
Theatre includes: Marathon (The Gate);
Second Hand Thunder (Tinderbox Theatre
Co.); Joyriders (Lyric, Belfast).
Television includes: David Copperfield, Rap at
the Door, Young Person's Guide to Becoming
a Rockstar, Off the Walls, Rab C Nesbitt.
Film includes: To End All Wars, The Last
Minute, County Kilburn, The Trench, Titanic
Town, Circus, Two Days in Spring, Cluck.
Ciaran was the recipient of the Kenneth
Branagh Renaissance Award (June 1997), and
in his year won the Gold Medal at RSAMD
1998.

Sophie Okonedo
For the Royal Court: Been So Long, Serious Money.
Other theatre includes: Troilus and Cressida, Money (RNT); Arabian Nights (Young Vic); His Lordship's Fancy (Gate); A Jovial Crew, The Odyssey, Tamburlaine the Great, The Changeling (RSC); 900 Oneonta (Old Vic).
Television includes: Never Never, In Defence, Staying Alive, Deep Secrets, Murder Most Horrid II, The Governor, The Age of Treason, Maria's Child.
Film includes: This Year's Love, The Jackal, Go Now, Ace Ventura II, Miss Queencake, Richard II, Timbuktu.
Radio includes: Pocahontas.

Johanna Town (lighting designer)
Johanna has been Head of Lighting for the Royal Court since 1990 and has designed extensively for the company during this time. Productions include: Under the Blue Sky, Mr Kolpert, Other People, Toast, The Kitchen, Faith Healer, Pale Horse, Search and Destroy, Women Laughing.
Other recent theatre designs include: Rita, Sue and Bob Too, A State Affair (Out of Joint/Soho Theatre); Arabian Nights (New Victory, New York); Ghost (Royal Exchange Theatre); Our Lady of Sligo (Irish Repertory Theatre, New York/RNT/Out of Joint); Some Explicit Polaroids, Drummers (Out of Joint); Rose (RNT/Broadway); Little Malcolm (Hampstead/West End); Our Country's Good (Young Vic/Out of Joint); Blue Heart (Royal Court/Out of Joint/New York).
Opera Includes: Tobias and the Angel (Almeida Opera Festival); La Boheme, Die Fledermaus (MTL).

Dawn Walton (assistant director)
For the Royal Court: Fireface, Breath, Boom, Been So Long.
As assistant director: Tamagotchi Heaven (Edinburgh Fringe Festival '98); Hansel and Gretel (Theatre Royal Stratford East).
For the Royal Court as director: Drag-On (Exposure Young Writers 2000), Breakpoint, The Shining (Young Writers' Programme) .
Other theatre includes: Splinters (Talawa Theatre Company).

Richard Wilson (director)
Associate Director of the Royal Court.
For the Royal Court: Mr Kolpert (for which he won TMA Award for Best Theatre Director), Toast, Four, God's Second in Command, Other Worlds, Heaven and Hell; A Wholly Healthy Glasgow, Women Laughing (both originally at the Royal Exchange, Manchester).
Other theatre includes: Four Knights in Knaresborough (New Vic Workshop for Tricycle); Tom & Clem (tour and West End); Simply Disconnected (Chichester); The Lodger (Hampstead /Royal Exchange, Manchester); Imagine Drowning, President Wilson in Paris, Lenz (Hampstead); Prin (Lyric Hammersmith); An Inspector Calls (Royal Exchange, Manchester); View of Kabul, Commitments (Bush); Teeth 'n' Smiles (Oxford Playhouse).
Television includes: Changing Step, A Wholly Healthy Glasgow, Under The Hammer, Remainder Man, Commitments.
Richard Wilson has many other credits for theatre, film and television as both an actor and a director.

THE ENGLISH STAGE COMPANY AT THE ROYAL COURT

The English Stage Company at the Royal Court opened in 1956 as a subsidised theatre producing new British plays, international plays and some classical revivals.

The first artistic director George Devine aimed to create a writers' theatre, 'a place where the dramatist is acknowledged as the fundamental creative force in the theatre and where the play is more important than the actors, the director, the designer'. The urgent need was to find a contemporary style in which the play, the acting, direction and design are all combined. He believed that 'the battle will be a long one to continue to create the right conditions for writers to work in'.

Devine aimed to discover 'hard-hitting, uncompromising writers whose plays are stimulating, provocative and exciting'. The Royal Court production of John Osborne's Look Back in Anger in May 1956 is now seen as the decisive starting point of modern British drama, and the policy created a new generation of British playwrights. The first wave included John Osborne, Arnold Wesker, John Arden, Ann Jellicoe, N F Simpson and Edward Bond. Early seasons included new international plays by Bertolt Brecht, Eugène Ionesco, Samuel Beckett, Jean-Paul Sartre and Marguerite Duras.

The theatre started with the 400-seat proscenium arch Theatre Downstairs, and then in 1969 opened a second theatre, the 60-seat studio Theatre Upstairs. Productions in the Theatre Upstairs have transferred to the West End, such as Conor McPherson's The Weir, Kevin Elyot's My Night With Reg and Ariel Dorfman's Death and the Maiden. The Royal Court also co-produces plays which have transferred to the West End or toured internationally, such as Sebastian Barry's The Steward of Christendom and Mark Ravenhill's Shopping and Fucking (with Out of Joint), Martin McDonagh's The Beauty Queen Of Leenane (with Druid Theatre Company), Ayub Khan-Din's East is East (with Tamasha Theatre Company, and now a feature film).

Since 1994 the Royal Court's artistic policy has again been vigorously directed to finding and producing a new generation of playwrights. The writers include Joe Penhall, Rebecca Prichard, Michael Wynne, Nick Grosso, Judy Upton, Meredith Oakes, Sarah Kane, Anthony Neilson, Judith Johnson, James Stock, Jez Butterworth, Marina Carr, Simon Block, Martin McDonagh, Mark Ravenhill, Ayub Khan-Din, Tamantha Hammerschlag, Jess Walters, Che Walker, Conor McPherson, Simon Stephens, Richard Bean, Roy

photo: Andy Chopping

Williams, Gary Mitchell, Mick Mahoney, Rebecca Gilman, Christopher Shinn, Kia Corthron, David Gieselmann, Marius von Mayenburg and David Eldridge. This expanded programme of new plays has been made possible through the support of A.S.K Theater Projects, the Jerwood Charitable Foundation, the American Friends of the Royal Court and many in association with the Royal National Theatre Studio.

In recent years there have been record-breaking productions at the box office, with capacity houses for Jez Butterworth's Mojo, Sebastian Barry's The Steward of Christendom, Martin McDonagh's The Beauty Queen of Leenane, Ayub Khan-Din's East is East, Eugène Ionesco's The Chairs, David Hare's My Zinc Bed and Conor McPherson's The Weir, which transferred to the West End in October 1998 and ran for nearly two years at the Duke of York's Theatre.

The newly refurbished theatre in Sloane Square opened in February 2000, with a policy still inspired by the first artistic director George Devine. The Royal Court is an international theatre for new plays and new playwrights, and the work shapes contemporary drama in Britain and overseas.

REBUILDING THE ROYAL COURT

In 1995, the Royal Court was awarded a National Lottery grant through the Arts Council of England, to pay for three quarters of a £26m project to completely rebuild our 100-year old home. The rules of the award required the Royal Court to raise £7.6m in partnership funding. The building has been completed thanks to the generous support of those listed below. We are particularly grateful for the contributions of over 5,700 audience members.

If you would like to support the ongoing work of the Royal Court, please contact the Development Department on 020 7565 5050.

ROYAL COURT
DEVELOPMENT BOARD
Elisabeth Murdoch (Chair)
Jonathan Cameron (Vice Chair)
Timothy Burrill
Anthony Burton
Jonathan Caplan QC
Joyce Hytner
Dany Khosrovani
Feona McEwan
Michael Potter
Sue Stapely
Charlotte Watcyn Lewis

PRINCIPAL DONOR
Jerwood Foundation

WRITERS CIRCLE
Sky
The Cadogan Estate
Carillon/Schal
News International plc
Pathé
The Eva and Hans K Rausing Trust
The Rayne Foundation
Garfield Weston Foundation

DIRECTORS CIRCLE
The Esmée Fairbairn Charitable Trust
The Granada Group plc

ACTORS CIRCLE
Edward C Cohen & The Blessing Way Foundation
Ronald Cohen & Sharon Harel-Cohen
Quercus Charitable Trust
The Basil Samuel Charitable Trust
The Trusthouse Charitable Foundation
The Woodward Charitable Trust

SPECIFIC DONATIONS
The Foundation for Sport and the Arts for Stage System
John Lewis Partnership plc for Balcony
City Parochial Foundation for Infra Red Induction Loops and Toilets for Disabled Patrons
RSA Art for Architecture Award Scheme for Antoni Malinowski Wall Painting

STAGE HANDS CIRCLE
Abbey National Charitable Trust
Anonymous
Miss P Abel Smith
The Arthur Andersen Foundation
Associated Newspapers Ltd
The Honorable M L Astor Charitable Trust
Rosalind Bax
Character Masonry Services Ltd
Elizabeth Corob
Toby Costin
Double O Charity
The D'Oyly Carte Charitable Trust
Thomas & Simone Fenton
Lindy Fletcher
Michael Frayn
Susan & Richard Hayden
Mr R Hopkins
Roger Jospé
William Keeling
Lex Service plc
Miss A Lind-Smith
The Mactaggart Third Fund
Fiona McCall
Mrs Nicola McFarland
Mr J Mills
The Monument Trust
Jimmy Mulville & Denise O'Donoghue
David Murby
Michael Orr
William Poeton CBE & Barbara Poeton
Angela Pullen
Mr & Mrs JA Pye's Charitable Settlement
Ruth & Richard Rogers
Ann Scurfield
Ricky Shuttleworth
Brian Smith
The Spotlight
Mr N Trimble
Lionel Wigram Memorial Trust
Madeline Wilks
Richard Wilson
Mrs Katherine Yates

DESIGN TEAM
Haworth Tompkins Architects
Tony Hudson
Theatre Projects Consultants
Schal Construction Management
Price & Myers
Max Fordham & Partners
Paul Gillieron Acoustic Design
Mark Henderson
The Peter Burholt Partnership
Centre for Accessible Environments
Citex Bucknall Austin
Arnold Project Services
Drivers Jonas
Michael Gallie & Partners
Montressor Partnership

THE
ARTS
COUNCIL
OF ENGLAND

PROGRAMME SUPPORTERS

The Royal Court (English Stage Company Ltd) receives its principal funding from the London Arts Board. It is also supported financially by a wide range of private companies and public bodies and earns the remainder of its income from the box office and its own trading activities. The Royal Borough of Kensington & Chelsea gives an annual grant to the Royal Court Young Writers' Programme and the London Boroughs Grants Committee provides project funding for a number of play development initiatives.

This year the Jerwood Charitable Foundation continues to support new plays by new playwrights with the fifth series of Jerwood New Playwrights. Since 1993 the A.S.K. Theater Projects of Los Angeles has funded a Playwrights' Programme at the theatre. Bloomberg Mondays, a continuation of the Royal Court's reduced price ticket scheme, is supported by Bloomberg. Sky has also generously committed to a two-year sponsorship of the Royal Court Young Writers' Festival.

Royal Court Registered Charity number 231242.

TRUSTS AND FOUNDATIONS
American Friends of the Royal Court Theatre
The Bulldog Princep Theatrical Fund
Gerald Chapman Fund
Cultural Foundation Deutsche Bank
The Genesis Foundation
The Goldsmiths Company
Jerwood Charitable Foundation
The John Lyons Charity
Laura Pels Foundation
Quercus Charitable Trust
The Peggy Ramsay Foundation
The Peter Sharp Foundation
Royal Victoria Hall Foundation
The Trusthouse Charitable Foundation

MAJOR SPONSORS
A.S.K. Theater Projects
AT&T
Barclays plc
Bloomberg
Sky
Credit Suisse First Boston
Francis Finlay
Lever Brothers & Elida Fabergé (through Arts & Business New Partners)
Marks and Spencer
Royal College of Psychiatrists
Virgin Atlantic

BUSINESS MEMBERS
Agnès b
Cartier
Goldman Sachs International
Laporte plc
Lazard Brothers & Co. Ltd
Lee and Pembertons
Lever Brothers & Elida Fabergé
Mask
McCABES
Redwood Publishing
Simons Muirhead & Burton
Space NK
J Walter Thompson

INDIVIDUAL MEMBERS
Patrons
David H Adams
Advanpress
Katie Bradford
Mrs Alan Campbell-Johnson
Gill Carrick
Conway van Gelder
Chris Corbin
David Day
Greg Dyke
Thomas Fenton
Ralph A Fields

John Flower
Mike Frain
Edna & Peter Goldstein
Judy & Frank Grace
David Graham
Phil Hobbs
Homevale Ltd
JHJ & SF Lewis
Lex Service plc
Barbara Minto
Michael & Mimi Naughton
New Penny Productions Ltd
Martin Newson
AT Poeton & Son Ltd.
André Ptaszynski, Really
Useful Theatres
David Rowland
Sir George Russell
Bernard Shapero
Mr & Mrs Anthony Weldon
Richard Wilson
George & Moira Yip

Benefactors
Anastasia Alexander
Lesley E Alexander
Batia Asher
Elaine Mitchell Attias
Thomas Bendhem
Jody Berger
Keith & Helen Bolderson
Jeremy Bond
Mr & Mrs F H Bradley III
Mrs Elly Brook JP
Julian Brookstone
Yuen-Wei Chew
Carole & Neville Conrad
Coppard & Co.
Barry Cox
Curtis Brown Ltd
Deborah Davis
Zoe Dominic
Robyn Durie
Winston & Jean Fletcher
Claire & William Frankel
Nicholas Fraser
Robert Freeman
J Garcia
Beverley & Nathaniel Gee
Norman Gerard
Henny Gestetner OBE
Jacqueline & Jonathan Gestetner
Michael Goddard
Carolyn Goldbart
Sally Greene
Byron Grote
Hamilton Asper Management
Anna Home CBE
Amanda Howard Associates
ICM Ltd
Trevor Ingman
Lisa Irwin-Burgess

Peter Jones
Paul Kaju & Jane Peterson
Peter & Maria Kellner
Catherine Be Kemeny
Thomas & Nancy Kemeny
Diana King
Clico Kingsbury
CA Leng
Lady Lever
Colette & Peter Levy
Ian Mankin
Christopher Marcus
Nicola McFarland
James McIvor
Mr & Mrs Roderick R McManigal
Mae Modiano
Pat Morton
Joan Moynihan
Georgia Oetker
Paul Oppenheimer
Mr & Mrs Michael Orr
Pauline Pinder
Carol Rayman
Angharad Rees
John & Rosemarie Reynolds
John Ritchie
Bernice & Victor Sandelson
John Sandoe (Books) Ltd
Nicholas Selmes
Lois Sieff OBE
Peregrine Simon
David & Patricia Smalley
Brian D Smith
Max Stafford-Clark
Sue Stapely
Ann Marie Starr
Martha & Carl Tack
Anthony Wigram

AMERICAN FRIENDS
Founders
Victoria Elenowitz
Francis Finlay
Monica Gerard-Sharp
Jeanne Hauswald
The Carl C Icahn Family Foundation
Mary Ellen Johnson
Dany Khosrovani
Kay Koplovitz
Laura Pels Foundation
Stephen Magowan
Monica Menell-Kinberg PhD
Benjamin Rauch
Rory Riggs
Robert Rosenkranz

Gerald Schoenfeld, The Schubert Organisation

Patrons
Daniel Baudendistel & Charles Klein
Arthur Bellinzoni
Robert L & Janice Billingsley
Harry Brown
Catherine G Curran
Leni Darrow
Michael & Linda Donovan
Ursula & William Fairbairn
April Foley
Amanda Foreman
The Howard Gilman Foundation
Richard Grand
Sharon King Hoge
Maurice & Jean R Jacobs
Barbara Kafka
Sahra T Lese
Susan & Martin Lipton
Anne Locksley
Eleanor Margolies
Hamish & Georgone Maxwell
Kathleen O'Grady
Howard & Barbara Sloan
Margaret Jackson Smith
Mika Sterling
The Thorne Foundation

Benefactors
Tom Armstrong
Mr Mark Arnold
Elaine Attias
David Day
Richard & Rosalind Edelman
Abe & Florence Elenowitz
Paul Epstein
Richard & Linda Gelfond
Hiram & Barbara Gordon
Paul Hallingby
Jennifer CE Laing
Imelda Liddiard
Richard Medley & Maureen Murray
Lawrence & Helen Remmel
Robert Rosenberg
Harold Sanditen
Charles Whitman

LONDON ARTS

AWARDS FOR
THE ROYAL COURT

Ariel Dorfman's Death and the Maiden and John Guare's Six Degrees of Separation won the Olivier Award for Best Play in 1992 and 1993 respectively. Terry Johnson's Hysteria won the 1994 Olivier Award for Best Comedy, and also the Writers' Guild Award for Best West End Play. Kevin Elyot's My Night with Reg won the 1994 Writers' Guild Award for Best Fringe Play, the Evening Standard Award for Best Comedy, and the 1994 Olivier Award for Best Comedy. Joe Penhall was joint winner of the 1994 John Whiting Award for Some Voices. Sebastian Barry won the 1995 Writers' Guild Award for Best Fringe Play, the 1995 Critics' Circle Award and the 1997 Christopher Ewart-Biggs Literary Prize for The Steward of Christendom, and the 1995 Lloyds Private Banking Playwright of the Year Award. Jez Butterworth won the 1995 George Devine Award for Most Promising Playwright, the 1995 Writers' Guild New Writer of the Year Award, the Evening Standard Award for Most Promising Playwright and the 1995 Olivier Award for Best Comedy for Mojo. Phyllis Nagy won the 1995 Writers' Guild Award for Best Regional Play for Disappeared.

The Royal Court won the 1995 Prudential Award for Theatre and was the overall winner of the 1995 Prudential Award for the Arts for creativity, excellence, innovation and accessibility. The Royal Court Theatre Upstairs won the 1995 Peter Brook Empty Space Award for innovation and excellence in theatre.

Michael Wynne won the 1996 Meyer-Whitworth Award for The Knocky. Martin McDonagh won the 1996 George Devine Award, the 1996 Writers' Guild Best Fringe Play Award, the 1996 Critics' Circle Award and the 1996 Evening Standard Award for Most Promising Playwright for The Beauty Queen of Leenane. Marina Carr won the 19th Susan Smith Blackburn Prize (1996/7) for Portia Coughlan. Conor McPherson won the 1997 George Devine Award, the 1997 Critics' Circle Award and the 1997 Evening Standard Award for Most Promising Playwright for The Weir. Ayub Khan-Din won the 1997 Writers' Guild Award for Best West End Play, the 1997 Writers' Guild New Writer of the Year Award and the 1996 John Whiting Award for East is East. Anthony Neilson won the 1997 Writers' Guild Award for Best Fringe Play for The Censor.

At the 1998 Tony Awards, Martin McDonagh's The Beauty Queen of Leenane (co-production with Druid Theatre Company) won four awards including Garry Hynes for Best Director and was nominated for a further two. Eugene Ionesco's

The Chairs (co-production with Theatre de Complicite) was nominated for six Tony awards. David Hare won the 1998 Time Out Live Award for Outstanding Achievement and six awards in New York including the Drama League, Drama Desk and New York Critics Circle Award for Via Dolorosa. Sarah Kane won the 1998 Arts Foundation Fellowship in Playwriting. Rebecca Prichard won the 1998 Critics' Circle Award for Most Promising Playwright for Yard Gal.

Conor McPherson won the 1999 Olivier Award for Best New Play for The Weir. The Royal Court won the 1999 ITI Award for Excellence in International Theatre. Sarah Kane's Cleansed was judged Best Foreign Language Play in 1999 by Theater Heute in Germany. Gary Mitchell won the 1999 Pearson Best Play Award for Trust. Rebecca Gilman was joint winner of the 1999 George Devine Award and won the 1999 Evening Standard Award for Most Promising Playwright for The Glory of Living. Roy Williams and Gary Mitchell were joint winners of the George Devine Award 2000 for Most Promising Playwright for Lift Off and The Force of Change respectively. At the Barclays Theatre Awards 2000 presented by the TMA, Richard Wilson won the Best Director Award for David Gieselmann's Mr Kolpert and Jeremy Herbert won the Best Designer Award for Sarah Kane's 4.48 Psychosis.

In 1999, the Royal Court won the European theatre prize New Theatrical Realities, presented at Taormina Arte in Sicily, for its efforts in recent years in discovering and producing the work of young British dramatists.

ROYAL COURT BOOKSHOP

The bookshop offers a wide range of playtexts, theatre books, screenplays and art-house videos with over 1,000 titles.

Located in the downstairs BAR AND FOOD area, the bookshop is open Monday to Saturday, afternoons and evenings.

Many of the Royal Court Theatre playtexts are available for just £2 including the plays in the current season and recent works by David Hare, Conor McPherson, Martin Crimp, Sarah Kane, David Mamet, Phyllis Nagy, Gary Mitchell, Marina Carr, Martin McDonagh, Ayub Khan-Din, Jim Cartwright and Rebecca Prichard. We offer a 10% reduction to students on a range of titles.

Further information : 020 7565 5024

FOR THE ROYAL COURT

Royal Court Theatre
Sloane Square, London SW1W 8AS
Tel: 020 7565 5050 Fax: 020 7565 5001
info@royalcourttheatre.com
www.royalcourttheatre.com

Which company will produce ten new plays in the next three months?

the wire
Bold, innovative, and original writing
Saturday evenings from 18 November

90-93 FM BBC RADIO 3
www.bbc.co.uk/radio3

I JUST STOPPED BY TO SEE THE MAN

for Annabel Arden

Characters

JESSE, *black, 75*

DELLA, *black, 34*

KARL, *white, 31*

Place: a bare 'shotgun' house in a small town in the Mississippi Delta

Time: the summer of 1975

Act One

Scene One: the early hours of Friday morning

Scene Two: the early hours of Saturday morning

Act Two

Scene One: late morning, Saturday

Scene Two: the early hours of Sunday morning

At the time of going to press, rehearsals were not completed, so the text here may differ from that in performance

ACT ONE

Scene One

Blackout.

In the darkness, the applause and whistling of a stadium rock audience fades in. A voice nurtured in the English Home Counties but hijacked by the American South takes on the crowd. The voice belongs to KARL.

KARL (*voice-over*). Thank you. Thank you, Memphis. There was a man came from round this way. Man from the Mississippi Delta.

Some isolated squeals of recognition from the cognoscenti.

A man they still call The Man.

More general applause.

Yeah, right. We're gonna play a coupla things he wrote. In his memory. Or who knows, maybe just in his honour, right? (Who knows, who knows?)

Some yells of approval.

Yeah, let's leave it at honour. We'll play the blues for The Man.

And the crowd responds to an Absent Friend, the lead guitar sketches a slow four bar intro high up on the fretboard and the bass and drums crash in. Sound fades out, lights fade in.

A bare shotgun house in the Mississippi Delta. One door leads to a porch, the other to the rest of the house.

An old black man sits on a chair. In his hand he holds three quarters. He pitches the coins towards an ancient but lovingly preserved fedora which is set on a towel on the floor some ten feet away. He sings a hymn in a good baritone. His name is JESSE.

JESSE.
> He rose, he rose, he rose from the dead
> He rose, he rose, he rose from the dead
> He rose –

He stops singing abruptly. He has run out of coins. He gets up, retrieves the three quarters and returns to his chair. He starts pitching again, resuming singing at the same time.

> He rose, he rose, he rose from the dead
> He rose, he rose, he rose from the dead
> He rose from the dead –

Again, he gets up, retrieves the coins and resumes his position.

> He rose, he rose, he rose from the dead
> He rose, he rose, he rose from the dead
> He rose, he rose, he rose from the dead,

The third coin hits the hat.

And my Lord shall bear my Saviour home.

He's happy. He goes to the hat, flicks dust off it, puts it on his head, pockets the coins and sits in satisfaction. Some moments. He listens. Hears nothing. He takes the hat off. Then he stands and puts it back in its former position on the towel. He thinks for a few moments, then sets the hat two feet further back. He sits down and pitches another coin. It misses.

He rose, he rose, he rose from the –

He stops in mid pitch. He listens. He's heard a sound from a long way off. Gradually it gets louder. A car is approaching, a 1959 Rambler. The car stops close by. JESSE picks up the hat, hangs it on a hook on the wall, folds the towel away in a drawer, sits in the chair and waits, staring ahead.

The front door opens. DELLA, a handsome black woman in her early thirties comes in. She carries a shoulder bag and a brown paper bag full of shopping. Immediately she locks the door and secures it with two large bolts.

DELLA. So I get this customer. There have to be eighty covers in the diner. He's just arrived, two minutes tops, I'm passing his table, carrying in my head five different requests from the assembled infants, excuse me customers, a clean fork, a second bottle of Coors –

JESSE. This is tonight?

DELLA *unpacks her shopping into the fridge. Then she fixes a wholesome looking fruit and yoghurt snack in a bowl.*

DELLA. This is tonight, two raisin and nut pancakes, a bottle of undrinkable house red and an offer of marriage from the stinkiest raincoat I ever smelt, which somewhere in its depths hides a life-form, something way low down in the food chain – a motor insurance clerk or similar, and this guy –

JESSE. The insurance guy?

DELLA. No, the new guy, the one I'm passing, he goes: 'Excuse me miss, am I invisible?' And I think maybe it's one of those games where people pretend to be goblins and he has, perhaps, had the gift of invisibility conferred on him by some internal wizard and he is seeking my confirmation – like: 'What, oh my God who said that, did the ketchup speak to me?' And then I realise, no this is humour, this is acerbic humour with a purpose. 'Am I invisible?' means, I have been sitting in a crowded restaurant for ninety seconds and no one has yet rushed up to check my diaper.

JESSE. 'Am I invisible?'

DELLA. I go: 'Excuse me?' He says: 'Can you see me? Can you see me or not? If you can see me, bring me a menu.'

JESSE. This is what, young guy, old guy –

DELLA *comes to the table and eats.*

DELLA. White guy. And I think, O.K. since we are playing out this exchange at advanced level, I reply: 'No, no that's not the question, the question is 'Can *you* see *me*?'' The brow furrows –

JESSE. The troubled brow, yes indeed, the mark on the forehead –

DELLA. You could sow corn in those furrows –

JESSE. 'Though you make them blossom in the morning that you sow; yet the harvest will flee away in a day of grief and incurable pain.'

DELLA. 'Can you see me? Can you see me as anything but a pair of black hands, a pair of black feet to bring you a menu. When I'm not wearing this uniform, can you even see me at all? If I were bleeding in a gutter would you even turn your face towards me –

JESSE. 'And he laid him down upon his bed, and turned away his face, and would eat no bread.'

DELLA. And then I think, no, I just overdid that. The scoop I am laying this on with is a couple of sizes too large and I will get it back with interest and sure enough he goes: 'Bring me the goddamn menu and quit your sass.' And I go: 'Oh why sir, there you are. I can see you now, you were really there all the time.'

JESSE. 'You were there all the time'. That's good enough. I'd score that a win to you on points.

DELLA. A knockout.

JESSE. I make it points.

DELLA. Thursdays I hate. Assholes winding up their nuts for the weekend. Traffic. And the Thursday special: 'Excuse me was I once a chicken, and even if I was, did I ever go to Maryland?'

JESSE. Lotta traffic Thursdays, Memphis?

Pause. Perhaps they've stumbled upon a conversational avenue which both would prefer to avoid.

DELLA. Maybe just tonight.

JESSE. I ain't been Memphis a dozen year or more. Nineteen sixty-two, sixty-three.

DELLA. I told you there'd be traffic tonight.

JESSE (*beat*). Oh sure. Well I had myself kind of a curious conversation too.

DELLA. You go to church?

JESSE. Yes I did, I took a walk up by the church.

DELLA. That's not takin' a walk, Pop. You could hit the church from that chair with a biscuit.

JESSE. I done took a walk by the church, and I went in and I prayed and when I come out, I'm feeling good and there's Alice Walcott, she's on her way in to pray and she sees me comin' out *from* prayin' and you know what she says?

DELLA. She's gonna put in a personal word for you with the Lord.

JESSE. No such thing. She says, you know something. When your daughter come back to live with you last year, we all wasn't so sure at first –

DELLA. We all?

JESSE. All her gossip women. With the big eyeglasses. They all got eyeglasses like goldfish bowls. She says we all ain't so sure. We don't know if this is your daughter, or you done took yourself a new wife. How do you like that? Seventy-five years old, she thinks I took me a new wife.

DELLA. I've seen it done.

JESSE. I tell her, shoot, that dog's hunting days is long gone.

DELLA. Gone, maybe. Long gone I say no.

JESSE. She goes: 'We done thought that old dog had caught a new rabbit. Maybe bit off more than it could chew.'

DELLA. She said that.

JESSE. Yes she did.

DELLA. Shame on her.

JESSE. I said I was too old to get caught that way. No devil woman gonna jump me. I told her: 'That's why I took a house at the cross road, so you can spot trouble comin' in all directions.'

DELLA. Pretty free with their mouths, those old bible beaters.

JESSE. All four directions. That was my day.

DELLA. Busy, busy.

Pause.

JESSE. Your guy, you know, he's got a point. I hate that, you go someplace to eat they don't acknowledge your presence.

DELLA. That's different, you're talking about black guy in a white place, no one takes notice, he's talking white guy in a mixed place.

JESSE. I been black guy, black place – still happens. I want people to see me.

DELLA. You want what?

JESSE. I'm talkin' bout the days when I would go into a diner. Days when I would go anyplace. I wish you would quit pullin' me up on that. When I talk about what I do, what I want, what I think, I'm talkin' bout what I used to do, used to want, used to think. I know I don't do nothin' no more. I know I just walk to the church and back. Just humour the way a person talks and don't give me none of that 'You want what?' –

DELLA. I'm saying nothing.

JESSE. There's things what's past. And things what's now. I know the difference. And I am content.

DELLA. Well if that's fine by you.

JESSE. I am content.

DELLA. Then that's fine by you.

DELLA *clears up her bowl, rinses it under the tap and places it on the side.*

JESSE. You know I heard something on the radio today.

DELLA. You don't listen to the radio.

JESSE. I listened today. They played a tune by Blind Lemon Jefferson.

DELLA. Why were you listening to the radio?

JESSE. They played 'See that my grave is kept clean'. Must be fifty years back he laid that thing down. And here I am sittin' in this chair listenin' to him singin' it today.

DELLA. That's how it works.

JESSE. Been *in* his grave forty-five years or more. Heard that and had him on my mind all day.

DELLA. That's good for you, Pop. I wasn't saying anything different.

JESSE. Did I tell you, I worked with him when I was seventeen, leading him around?

DELLA. Yeah, I heard that.

JESSE. You know, Blind Lemon, he always carried a gun.

DELLA (*beat*). Yeah?

JESSE. Had a pearl handle.

DELLA. Blind Lemon carried a gun?

JESSE. Can make an individual nervous, you understand. You got a blind man on a leash, and he's packing a forty-five, keeps you pretty ginger. He used to say 'Hey, boy, it's quiet, where you takin' me?' I said 'I'm goin' some place there's no one for you to shoot at.' He goes: 'Hell, you won't be no safer, I'm just as like to shoot at nothin'.' That was not what you call a steady job, three months was about my fill of that class of behaviour. (*Pause.*) He got rich, bought two cars, to be driven around in. I caught up with him one time, Chicago, just when I was gettin' known. I says to him: 'Hey, Blind Lemon, what's with you having two cars?' He says: 'Jesse, I don't like my other chauffeur.' (*Pause.*) And he was right, 'cuz Blind Lemon died in his other car, had a heart attack one Chicago winter, and the body was discovered all alone. That chauffeur had walked. Left him to freeze, freeze like a big iceberg till the cops found him. Blind Lemon Jefferson.

DELLA. That's history for you.

JESSE. What you sayin'?

DELLA. History always blames the chauffeur. He could have been walking to get help, lost his way in a blizzard. Could have been Blind Lemon sacked him first, then had the heart attack, fit of remorse.

JESSE. I set eyes on that chauffeur, Della. He was a man of bad character. He was a man sent from the Devil.

DELLA. Blues singer with two chauffeurs deserves what he gets.

Pause.

JESSE. 'Am I invisible?' You say your diner man is wrong to ask that question. But I wonder, Della. I do wonder that myself sometimes.

DELLA. Pop, you made yourself invisible. What do you expect.

JESSE. There were circumstances.

DELLA. You let the world believe you were dead, you can't expect to be visible after that.

JESSE. I read my obituary. Chicago Tribune. I liked it. I thought, hell, I can't do no better than that, I'll go with the Trib, quit while I'm ahead.

DELLA. You did not think that.

JESSE. I wouldn't swear now to know what I thought and what I did not.

DELLA. You walked away.

JESSE. Only thing I do say is this. I hear 'bout your invisible man tonight and I'm thinking. Hell, that's not such a dumb question, that ain't even a discourteous question.

DELLA. Leave it, Pop.

JESSE. You look at yourself and ask the question over. 'Am I invisible?' 'Cuz why else, when you got college degrees all up your arm are you servin' a person like that in a Memphis diner? Who's the dumb one here? Who's harder to see of the two of you?

DELLA. Pop, you're sitting here in a bare-wall shotgun shack, five dollars in your pocket and that English faggot band is up the road in Memphis playing your songs to that big, big crowd.

JESSE. Are they faggots?

DELLA. I don't know.

JESSE. That's just being English.

DELLA. Maybe so.

JESSE. I heard them on that radio today too. You know, I was surprised, 'cuz they play pretty good.

DELLA. They sell a million records of a song you wrote back in 1931. You got fifteen dollars for it. What have they got?

JESSE. Dead man can't renegotiate his contracts. That I do know.

Pause.

DELLA. Maybe we'd best just not talk when I come back.

JESSE. Della, I like to talk with you.

DELLA. Well, all we did is talk about what happened today –

JESSE. O.K. I won't talk about you waitin' table if you don't talk to me 'bout bein' dead.

DELLA. Doesn't leave a lot –

JESSE. No, but we'll find some way –

DELLA. – some way of scratching each other's faces.

JESSE. Scratchin' ain't bad. You just gotta stop –

DELLA. Before the blood flows.

JESSE. No, *when* the blood flows. You scratch, you draw blood, you quit.

DELLA. Family life.

JESSE. Successful family life.

DELLA. Like we'd know.

Pause.

JESSE. Yeah. Well, I'll go to bed. Maybe I'll sleep.

DELLA. Try to sleep, Pop.

He kisses her head.

JESSE. Always try. But it ain't a tryin' type of activity. Goodnight.

DELLA. Goodnight.

JESSE. Maybe I'll just hear that old Blind Lemon in my head.

He goes out through the connecting door.

DELLA *is alone. She sits for a moment. She walks over to
her shoulder bag and brings it back to the armchair. She
looks inside. She brings out a thick black notebook and a
pack of cigarettes. She lights a cigarette. She opens the
notebook and starts to write in it. She writes feverishly for
a few moments. Then stops. She stares ahead.*

*She begins to cry. Some moments. She gets a grip on
herself. She stands, walks up and down, smoking.*

A knock at the door. DELLA *reacts with disproportionate
fear. She backs away, hanging on to the fridge, staring at
the door.*

More knocking, louder. DELLA *is immobilised with dread.
Silence. Perhaps the visitor has gone. She treads warily into
the centre of the room.*

A scraping at the window. Someone is trying to break in.
DELLA *can't decide what to do. A hand taps at the pane
with a stone.* DELLA *stares, unable to move.*

*The hand taps harder. The pane breaks. A hand curls round,
unlocks the window and lifts it.*

KARL *appears. He is white, just over thirty, chicken bone
thin, long dark hair, unnaturally pale face. He wears a long
batik scarf round his neck and carries a leather saddle bag.
He has style. Even when the fashions are bad he will look
good.*

*He is clearly out of his head on something. He straddles the
sill and climbs into the room making an awkward landing.
He stands, his hands over his eyes looking dazed.*

DELLA *stares at him. She smiles slightly. Whatever she was
afraid of, it is not this.*

KARL. Man, I got spots in front of my eyes.

DELLA. You got what?

KARL. I did something to my eyes man.

DELLA. Do I care? You've broken my window.

KARL. Must have jarred something, climbing in.

DELLA. You have an optic nerve in your ankle?

KARL. That's my life. Things get misplaced.

DELLA. What are you on?

KARL. Am I in the right place?

DELLA. I would say not.

He looks at her for the first time.

KARL. My name is Karl –

DELLA. I know who you are. How was Memphis?

KARL. Sorry?

DELLA. Your gig. How did it go?

KARL. Oh right. Who are you?

DELLA. How was the gig?

KARL. Cool.

DELLA. Are you faggots, just English or both?

KARL. Depends what town we're in.

DELLA. Where are you tomorrow?

KARL. Baton Rouge.

DELLA. Then I'd be careful.

KARL. Thanks for the tip.

DELLA. I'm Della and you've just broken into my house.

KARL. It wasn't personal.

DELLA. It was criminal.

KARL. Slightly criminal. It came to me, up on stage –

DELLA. You smashed my window.

KARL. I'm sorry, man. Here look.

He rummages in his pockets.

DELLA. Are you offering me money?

KARL. You're in luck. I don't usually carry money on tour.
But I really like dollars. The way they all look the same but
the numbers are different. So I stay well stashed. Dollars are
cool. Here.

He hands her a fistful of money.

DELLA. This is too much.

KARL. Get a good one.

DELLA. There's five hundred dollars here.

KARL. See, I was up on stage and I had this –

> *He has seen the guitar above the mantelpiece. He stands staring at it, awestruck.*

> That's his guitar. The Martin D-45. (*Pause.*) This is the place, isn't it?

> DELLA *sits down and lights a cigarette.*

KARL. Isn't it?

DELLA. Shit.

KARL. This is his place, yeah?

DELLA. Here comes another one.

KARL. Another one?

DELLA. Did he live here? Is that really *the* guitar? Are there photos? And, the number one question –

KARL. Is he still alive?

DELLA. That's the one.

KARL. Is he still alive?

DELLA. They always ask that one.

KARL. Well?

DELLA. Do you have any of his records?

KARL. I got all his records.

DELLA. What does it say on them?

KARL. It says he died in a car crash in 1961.

DELLA. Karl, I say this to you: 'Believe the sleeves.'

KARL. The circumstances were mysterious.

DELLA. Guitarists always die mysteriously. It's their way of being interesting. One day you'll catch yourself doing it.

KARL. How do you know Jesse Davidson is dead?

DELLA. I'm his daughter.

Pause.

KARL. Right. Della. He has six children.

DELLA. Correct.

KARL. You're the only legitimate one.

DELLA. Oh shit, you took the degree. When's his birthday?

KARL. Seventeenth of November.

DELLA. The Master's degree.

KARL. Good to meet you.

DELLA. I was at the funeral. He's dead. I know. Trust me.

KARL. I read the casket was closed.

DELLA. Not to me it wasn't. He was badly disfigured but it was him.

KARL *sits down. He's a little deflated.*

KARL. I had this vision up on stage. There was a quart of Jack Daniels going round the five of us. Then someone passed me a pipe, I don't know what was in it. It came together in my mind, we did a Robert Johnson tune. I started getting these flashes. The Man's face. That guitar. A road I'd been down before. A house at a crossroads.

DELLA. You just struck lucky?

KARL. We've been here a week. Every spare moment, I get the car to come out here. Into the Delta. Sniff round the little towns, asks questions, look at the landscape, clues in the lyrics.

DELLA. I hate it when they find clues in the lyrics.

KARL. I stopped by here last night. Some guy in a gas station said something. 'There's an old black man I pass a mile down the road.' I had a feeling. But he didn't know what house.

Pause.

DELLA. I don't like to disappoint you but he was in the car with his wife when it crashed.

KARL. Angela.

DELLA. She'd wanted him to give up playing, singing. He was sixty. She thought that was enough. Wanted him to take a job in a bar or something. He was on his way to a gig. She wasn't going to go, changed her mind at the last minute. He turned the car over.

KARL. Station wagon.

DELLA. All right. Station wagon. Thing is this, Karl. I have my own life and it's here, and though I keep the guitar and all, because it was his house and he was my Daddy . . . I don't really give a shit about –

KARL. Trainspotters like me.

DELLA. Especially this late at night. You understand?

KARL. The guitar wasn't found in the station wagon. And he carried it in a big coffin case, solid, wouldn't have been smashed. He was on his way to a gig. Some people said the cops stole it. But there it is on your wall.

DELLA *lights a cigarette.*

DELLA. It was a regular gig with a quartet in a bar, big barn of a place. He had to play an electric with them to be heard. A pale blue Gibson Thunderbird since you ask. It was the house instrument. Belonged to the owner. He never put the Martin in the car.

KARL *stands, an English gent sobering up.*

KARL. I'm sorry. I've been out of line.

DELLA. Yes you have, Karl.

KARL. Can I call you?

DELLA. Well look, why don't I call you?

KARL. We're at the Peabody. There's a password. You say: 'Muddy Waters' and they put you through.

DELLA. Well of course.

KARL. Hey, man, I'm sorry about the window.

DELLA. It's O.K. about the window.

KARL. No, I'm sorry.

DELLA. You paid for the window.

KARL. You come see us, Baton Rouge? Call me tomorrow, I'll put you on the door.

DELLA. O.K.

KARL. Be an honour. Bring a friend.

DELLA. Sure.

KARL. Long tour, you know.

KARL is at the door. He turns the handle and opens it. JESSE appears at the connecting door. He's dressed in a long striped robe.

JESSE. Della. What I say to you before, hell I don't mean that.

KARL stares at JESSE. KARL closes the front door and leans against it.

KARL. What he said to you before. He didn't mean it.

JESSE notices KARL. JESSE looks hard at KARL. KARL stares at JESSE. They both know immediately who the other is.

Long pause. KARL takes the cigarette from DELLA. He draws on it hard.

KARL. O.K. I'm relaxed about this. I can handle this.

JESSE stares at KARL as he pulls on DELLA's cigarette.

JESSE. Are you midnight creepin' around my daughter, boy?

KARL. My name's Karl. I'm with an English band. We play the blues, well we started playing the blues, things got more . . . We did this gig in Memphis, the last of three nights. We had a hit with one of your songs. 'Shotgun Blues'. It went platinum, there was a lot of royalties. (*Beat.*) I think you might need to call your agent.

Pause.

I always loved your records. That's what got me going. The guitar, the blues. But I never been this part of the world before. First night, we finish the gig, we leave in the helicopter, the other guys go back to the hotel, I take the chopper on. Just to take a look at the Delta. We landed in some field. I'd sent my chauffeur on ahead. Climbed in. And off we go. The Delta by night. And we're passing little places and I'm going: 'Son House came from here, B. B. King from there, Muddy Waters down there, Willie Dixon . . . ' And then, round about dawn, I go like: 'You know if the theory is true, if The Man didn't die, then he'll be here. Wouldn't stay in Chicago. Too many people. He'd come back to somewhere he knows – not exactly where he came from, maybe forty, fifty, miles further north.' We drove back to the hotel. I got two rules for surviving tours: don't eat and don't sleep. Then you might make it. So I stayed up. Got a road map of the Delta. Put myself in your shoes. Where would I go? Where would I go if I were you? Made a short list. Yesterday evening, same shot. End of gig, the chopper, the motor. Drove around all night, all day. I kept thinking I'm so close, I can sense him. We came right past here. Tonight I'm up on stage. Robert Johnson number. I'm singing it and it hits me. Crossroads. That's where he'd go. He'd go to live at a crossroads. And this flashed through my mind. Gig ends, the chopper, the motor. I look at it. Four buildings. A church, a used car lot, a very neat house. And this one. It had to be. It had to be. And it was.

JESSE *stands for a moment. He goes to the broken window. He picks at the wreckage.*

JESSE. Will you observe the criminal times we have to endure? When I went to bed, this window was in perfect condition. (*Beat.*) Am I supposed to know who you are?

KARL. Like I said, I'm with this band –

JESSE. I heard that. But it didn't mean nothin' to me. I don't listen to that stuff. You think I go out, buy your records –

KARL. I –

JESSE. I don't even got a music machine no more. I don't hear no radio. I don't care you make a lot of money outa me. I'm a dead man, you understand.

KARL. I just thought –

JESSE. And what's this shit about a cross road?

KARL. Crossroads. It's the great myth. The myth of the blues.

JESSE. Don't believe I ever heard it.

KARL. It's the story they tell. About Robert Johnson. And about you. You were a young man, you wanted to play, you worked at it but there was something missing. You heard this story. From a witch doctor. You decided to give it a go. You went to a crossroads at midnight with your guitar. You played a song. Then you heard footsteps behind you. You kept right on playing. The footsteps stop. It's the Devil. He taps you on your shoulder. You hand him your guitar. He tunes it for you. Hands it back, walks away, you mustn't turn around. And immediately you can play. You can play like nobody else. Only you owe him your soul. You trade your soul to the Devil so you can play the blues.

JESSE. And you believe that?

KARL. That's the story they tell.

JESSE. I know they tell it. I wanted to hear you tell it. And now I'm questioning you. Do you have any belief in it?

KARL. Yeah. I believe it.

Pause. JESSE *is grave. Then he turns to* DELLA. *He grins at her. She laughs.* JESSE *laughs. They both laugh at* KARL.

JESSE. He believes it.

DELLA. They like that story.

JESSE. Yeah, they do, lot of white folks used to come to me, with that story. I like to hear you folks tell that one.

DELLA. White folks, very superstitious.

JESSE. They is very superstitious folks.

DELLA. They take to that stuff, that Devil stuff –

JESSE. Della, get to bed.

Pause.

DELLA. What did you say?

JESSE. I'm going to speak with this gentleman here. I want you to get to bed.

A moment. KARL *watches* DELLA *carefully. She's a bit surprised by* JESSE's *firmness.*

DELLA. Well. I suppose you get what you want.

JESSE. Nope. But I do this time.

DELLA. Just this time. All right. Goodnight.

DELLA *goes.*

JESSE. Sit down.

KARL *sits.*

Now then. I wanna ask you some questions. Where you from?

KARL. Surrey.

JESSE. Surrey, England.

KARL. Yeah, Surrey England.

JESSE. And what goes down there?

KARL. A lot of stockbrokers sleep there. When they're awake they work in their gardens.

JESSE. Stock (*beat*) brokers. What they grow?

KARL. Stuff. Flowers. Lobelias are big.

JESSE. Lotta lobelias.

KARL. It's the same all over the home counties, but Surrey –

JESSE. The home counties?

KARL. It's like a bit in the corner of England. They call it the home counties.

JESSE. Sounds bad for the other counties.

KARL. You could say that.

JESSE. What are they sayin' – those other counties, you can't be at home in them –

KARL. No –

JESSE. You can't make a home in them?

KARL. Not exactly –

JESSE. I don't get it. Home counties –

KARL. It's just a phrase –

JESSE. Gonna ask you somethin'. If you're from Surrey, Home Counties, England –

KARL. Uh huh?

JESSE. Why you talk that way?

KARL. What way?

JESSE. I met folks from England. I never been to England, but I heard some that come over here and I hear them in the movies. They don't none of them talk like you.

KARL. I talk like I talk, man.

JESSE. I know that. I can hear you talking like you talk. What I wanna know is how you come to invent that way of talking.

KARL. What way's that?

JESSE. You talk like you got dropped from a plane into the Deep South of the United States of America for a couple of hours and couldn't get it out of your head.

KARL. That's about right. In 1961 I heard an Elmore James album three times in a row, straight off. Two hours in the Mississippi Delta. I was in heaven.

JESSE. You didn't have to work in it.

KARL. You didn't have to live in Surrey. It's more subtle than slavery. It's pebbledash house fronts and quiet and clocks that chime the quarters. To survive, you have to invent stuff. You're like: 'The Luftwaffe hit the back bedroom last night and we're digging Granny out of the rubble.' It becomes a habit. Then when you get to fifteen, sixteen, it strikes you. Instead of inventing little bits here and there, you invent the whole thing. You invent a new you. You change your way of dressing, your hair, your attitudes. And when you open your mouth. A different sound comes out.

JESSE. Escape into yourself.

KARL. Yeah.

JESSE. I can comprehend that. See, when you worked in the
cotton fields, you worked from 'can' to 'can't'. 'Can see'
start working. 'Can't see' stop working. Mississippi summer
that's five in the morning till ten at night. Nineteen twenty-
one. Times was so hard you couldn't cut 'em with a Kaiser
blade. I was out, number seven cut one morning, could have
been nine, ten o'clock I don't know. I heard my Pal Jimmy
singing a hymn: 'I can see Him no more on this earth'. He
weren't a religious man, you understand, he's telling
everyone that the overseer ain't around and you could stand,
stretch your back a little. And I did that and I looked around
at the field and at my mule. Stood doin' nothin' for near on
a minute, starin' at that old mule, he knows somethin's up,
goddamn mule turns, stares at me, like to say: 'What's goin'
down here?' And I'm like you, I gone somewhere inside
myself. And I think who's better off here, the mule or me?
I consider and I answer in favour of the mule on account
he's like to be dead in a couple of years. And I just start to
walk. I walk away. From the mule, from the cotton field,
from Jimmy who's singin', 'Come back my redeemer' but
I don't pay him no mind. I didn't plan nothin' and I hit a
time when every damn overseer is lookin' some place else.
I just walk away and I don't stop walking till I get to
Memphis Tennessee.

KARL. The escape. That's the big moment, man.

JESSE. But see where we're different. I think if you sing a
song about Atlanta, you got to have been to Atlanta. Sing
about climbin' aboard a box-car, to catch a ride you
understand, you got to have done that thing. Sing about
firing a shotgun at the man who's screwin' your wife . . .
See what I'm sayin'.

KARL. You said you never heard my music –

JESSE. I don't have to. I don't have to hear it 'cuz I know. You
want me to sing you somethin'?

KARL. Sure.

KARL's *eyes wander to the guitar on the wall.*

JESSE. No, I ain't takin' that guitar down. I ain't taken that off the wall in fourteen years. I'm gonna sing you a song I just wrote. You wanna hear it?

KARL. I wanna hear it.

JESSE. It's called: Surrey Blues.

Pause. JESSE *closes his eyes. He stamps his foot in time and sings out loud and clear.*

Down in the Home Counties,
Folks have to work so very hard.
Said down in them Homesick Counties
Folks have to work so very hard
Gotta broke my stocks all day
Then plant lobelias down in my yard.

JESSE *opens his eyes and stares at* KARL.

Didn't make any kind of sense did it? See what I'm sayin'. To sing the blues you got to know the blues. To sing the blues you got to have the blues.

KARL *smiles. He stands. He walks to the saddle bag and pulls out a quart of Jack Daniels. He picks a couple of glasses from the sink and plonks the bottle and glasses on the table. He takes off his Batik scarf and drapes it over the lamp so the room becomes darker, the light focused around the table. He sits.*

JESSE. What makes you think I like to drink this stuff?

KARL. I know what you like.

JESSE. You know what I liked when I was alive.

KARL *pours the bourbon. He drinks,* JESSE *doesn't.*

KARL. Why did you do it?

JESSE. I think a bunch of people would if they ever got the chance. I got the chance. I rather would have been dead, to speak the truth to you. But I took the next best thing.

KARL. And who knows?

JESSE. Della. And you.

KARL *weighs this.*

KARL. See this, Jesse. You made a certain sound. Then forty years later, that sound crosses the Atlantic. Settles in the English suburbs. I thought I was the only guy in Britain who knew about it. One day I'm on a train and I see another cat, my age, he's got a Muddy Waters album under his arm. I nearly proposed to him. Then I found out, there's hundreds of us. London, Newcastle, Liverpool, Glasgow. It meant more to us than it did to the kids here in the Delta. They're listening to some new shit, we're all saying, no man, go back, go back, find the root. We didn't live through what you lived through. But we knew what it was you were saying. First time I heard your voice, on an old gramophone, in a flat off the Fulham Road where I'd go and crash – escaping – I heard your voice and I thought 'This is it.' The blues is the blues for all time. You invented it. But we took it on and we knew straight off what the blues meant.

JESSE *drinks for the first time. Just a sip.*

JESSE. This is smoother than what I used to sell.

KARL. Well, this is legal, man.

JESSE. So what you come here for?

KARL. I had to know.

JESSE. And now you know.

KARL. You say you have to have the blues to sing the blues.

JESSE. That's the truth.

KARL. And you say someone like me can't really have the blues.

JESSE. That's what I believe.

KARL. So look at me and you. Is it better to sing the blues but not to have them. Or to have the blues and not sing them?

JESSE. I don't have no choice. Dead man can't sing.

KARL. I'm gonna give you a choice.

JESSE. I don't got no choice, boy.

KARL. We've been on tour, three months. Last two dates: Baton Rouge tomorrow. New Orleans the day after. This is the shot. End of the show, I go back on stage and introduce the encore. You. And you come on, the suit, the fedora, the guitar. And you play with the band. Three numbers and out. The back from the dead gig. Ten years time, people who were thousands of miles away will swear they were there. Are you in?

JESSE *looks at* KARL, *then drains the glass. He laughs.*

JESSE. What's the matter? Not selling enough records? Need me to give you all a lift?

KARL. The band has reached a certain point.

JESSE. A certain point.

KARL. Let's just leave it at that.

JESSE. You've come to a certain point. And you think all these white college kids are gonna take kindly to you bringing on some old nigger they never heard of.

KARL. They've heard, man –

JESSE. Some old nigger who ain't played for fourteen years, up on stage hollerin' about some girl who left him fifty years back.

KARL. I think that's just what they want to hear.

JESSE. Karl, I don't like to say this, but I think you are in trouble.

KARL. Trouble knows my address.

JESSE. I think you're in some bad trouble in your life and you think I can pull you out.

KARL. I'm cool, man.

JESSE. Well you had a question for me, I got a question for you.

KARL. Shoot.

JESSE. Here's my question: 'Is the Lord in your life?'

KARL. No. He's not. The Lord is not in my life.

JESSE. That's why you're in trouble. And that's why I won't play no blues no more. I won't play with you. Hell, I won't even pick up that guitar and sing 'Sweet Home Chicago.'

KARL. You could still play with Christ in your life.

JESSE. Karl. You maybe play the blues, you maybe even have the blues, but somehow you don't *get* the blues. This music gets deep down in your spirit. It's bad. You know what they call it –

KARL. The Devil's music.

JESSE. The Devil's music. You tell me when you come in, you believe that story of me and the Devil at the cross road. If you believe that, you gotta believe that the blues is sin. I believe that. I believe playin' the blues cost me everything that was good in my life. And now I don't have nothin'. 'Cept two things: my daughter and The Lord. And I ain't singin' no blues again for fear I lose them.

KARL. I hear what you say, Jesse. I don't agree with it, but I hear it.

JESSE. Well. I spoke my word on the subject. And it's my last word. It's late.

KARL. Yeah. (*Pause.*) Only thing is this: I know your secret. Just me and Della.

JESSE. You know my secret. You gonna tell anyone?

KARL. It's up to you.

JESSE. Hell, I don't want you to tell no one. I'd make you take an oath on the Holy Bible if I thought it meant a thing to you.

KARL. I won't tell anyone. If you let me come back tomorrow.

JESSE. Tomorrow?

KARL. Same time, same place.

JESSE. What for?

KARL. Talk some more. Drink some more.

JESSE. Unusual hours you keep.

KARL. I'm on what we call band time. It's different.

JESSE. Yeah? I remember band time. You keep track of the minutes but not the hours. It's like being old.

KARL. I guess.

JESSE. O.K. Go now. Come back tomorrow night.

KARL finishes his drink. Leaves the bottle behind. Picks up his bag. Goes to the door.

KARL. I'm gone.

JESSE. Yeah. Hey, man.

KARL. Yeah?

JESSE. Tomorrow, (*beat*) use the door.

KARL smiles. Then he's gone without looking back. JESSE pours another drink. He knocks it back. Some moments.

JESSE (*calling out*). Della! Della!

But no one comes. JESSE sits and stares ahead. The lights fade to

Blackout.

Scene Two

In the darkness another rock audience fades in.

KARL(*voice-over*). Awright now, Baton Rouge. D'you like the blues?

The crowd roar 'Yes.'

You ever hear of a player called Jesse Davidson?

Huge roars. Some shouts of 'The Man, The Man.'

They say he died. I say he lives on. What you say, Baton Rouge?

The crowd roars.

Lights up. The broken window is covered with a piece of cardboard. The sound of the gig is now emerging from a portable cassette player on the table. KARL stands over it, looking at JESSE who sits at the table listening impassively. DELLA lies on the sofa reading a newspaper. KARL hits the stop button.

KARL. What did you say yesterday?

JESSE. I forget.

KARL. About them not knowing you?

JESSE. I said maybe they wouldn't know me.

KARL. Some old nigger they never heard of.

JESSE. What?

KARL. That's what you said. Some old nigger they never heard of.

DELLA. He always says that.

KARL. Thank you. That's what you said.

JESSE. Maybe I did.

KARL. You know how many people I'm talking to there?

JESSE. I played big crowds.

DELLA. Did you ever.

JESSE. I played one time to twelve hundred people.

DELLA. Praise the Lord.

JESSE. Some place New York City, they pulled it down –

KARL. Jesse we're not talking twelve hundred.

DELLA. Pop, there'll be twelve hundred hamburger sellers.

JESSE. You got more than twelve hundred there?

KARL. Whole lot more.

DELLA. Pop, it's a football stadium.

JESSE. How many folks you got there?

KARL. Jesse, there's fifty-seven thousand people at that concert.

JESSE. Fifty-seven thousand?

KARL. Fifty-seven thousand people calling your name.

JESSE. I didn't know it was that much.

KARL. That's one gig. The whole tour, worldwide, you're talking about a couple of million people. Who know you.

JESSE. Two million people.

DELLA. And they're all white.

KARL. Tokyo?

DELLA. White to their souls.

JESSE (*cassette*). That's some machine there.

KARL. It's yours, Jesse, have it.

DELLA. Forget Tokyo. Talk Memphis. How many black kids are getting in at twenty bucks a shot?

JESSE. That's a *lotta* people.

KARL. We played three of your songs. They join in. They know the words.

DELLA. Well, he ain't exactly Paul Verlaine.

KARL. To them you're still The Man.

JESSE. You're easy to love when you're safe dead and gone.

KARL. Jesse, they want you.

JESSE *suddenly gets up and walks to the broken window.*

JESSE. Karl, why'd you come back?

KARL. I said I would. We cut a deal.

JESSE. Oh yeah?

KARL. Yes we did, Jesse. You said I could come back if I kept your secret. And I did. Didn't tell the band, didn't tell the crew, security, groupies –

DELLA. Hamburger sellers –

KARL. Anyone.

JESSE. Well we may have cut a deal. And we may have said certain things half-drunk. But you should know how I want it, Karl. I want to be left alone.

KARL. You dug those cats getting off on you.

JESSE. I don't care for that shit. I'm not like Big Bill Broonzy, lookin' for affection. I wanted a little fear, a little edge when I sang to a crowd. I never learned to play hillbilly songs and Carolina Moon. I just played the blues, played it straight

and hard and if they didn't like it, swell, 'cuz I didn't have
no love lost for them. That's why I lay doggo when the
college kids found them old timers, John Hurt, Skippy
James, brought 'em back and worshipped them. I did not
wish to be found. If they wanted me, they had my records.
I wasn't gonna be the court jester, the lovable old man.

DELLA. The lovable old black man.

JESSE. I didn't say anything about black.

DELLA. That's why I said it for you.

JESSE. You got children, Karl?

KARL. My lawyers say so.

JESSE. You wanna watch for the time they start telling you
what you think.

DELLA. I'm telling you what I think.

JESSE. You know I went to prison, Karl.

KARL. I know that.

JESSE. Five years in Parchman. I shot a man I didn't know
'cuz he was getting too friendly with my Angela. Saturday
night frolic. Blew the back off of his head with a thirty-
eight. Always carried a gun, them days, often used it.
Should have done twenty-five to life. But you know how it
goes. The guy I shot weren't important. He was only some
nigger, you understand. So I cut a deal. On the inside. Made
over a good slice of my earnings for the next five years.
See, that's the kind of personality I am. Kill one of my own
kind over nothin'. Then bribe the white jailers so I can walk
free. That's the type of person you're hopin' to associate
with. Type of person you're lookin' to present to them
college kids.

KARL. Jesse, I know that. They know that.

DELLA. Pop, it makes them love you all the more. It makes
you politically acceptable.

JESSE. Oh-ho, now listen up, here, Karl –

DELLA. You know it's the truth.

JESSE. – because this, what we're about to receive, is the pure gospel, you understand.

DELLA. I'm saying nothing.

JESSE. Go on, child. I paid for the book learnin' –

DELLA. Says who?

JESSE. – sowed the seeds, I wanna taste the fruit –

DELLA. Fuck you, Pop. I worked my eyes blind to get to college and when I get there, what stunt do you pull?

JESSE. I'd made you by then –

DELLA. You made me the little girl who loves her Daddy too much. And then you go pretend you're dead.

JESSE. See what I'm sayin', Karl. I'm a bad man through and through. I'm so bad that every woman I ever knowed betrayed me.

DELLA. And that's why those white folks would love you. Perfect black man of their dreams. Their grandfathers worked you to the bone in the plantations. Their fathers spat on your children in the streets. And then they steal your music and get rich on it. If you go up on that stage you'll betray your past: 'All those terrible things we did to him and he still comes out and sings to us.' It doesn't matter how bad a man you are, they will filter that out. 'O.K. He's rough, a little drunk, a little savage to his womenfolk. But that's our fault, that's how us whites made him grow up.' Play it as mean as you like, they'll turn you into a sweet old man.

JESSE. I don't know what you're excitin' yourself over, I ain't doin' the gig.

DELLA. They'll go: 'If only the niggers today were like him 'stead of being all uppity and setting fire to the ghettos.'

JESSE. They talk plantation who never saw plantation. They talk plantation who only read plantation.

JESSE *goes off through the door, right.*

DELLA. He won't do it.

KARL. We'll see.

DELLA. Yesterday he gave you the flat 'no'. Today he's gonna string you along. He's like a high school girl. He'll flirt, he'll show his legs but he won't put out. You got him fretting because you found him out alive. But he won't play.

KARL. Della, I need him bad.

DELLA. So what you going to do? Put the squeeze on him? Break the story that he's still alive?

KARL. I respect the guy.

DELLA. Then let him be.

KARL goes to the shelf. He pours a slug of whiskey. He seems momentarily depressed.

DELLA. Know what I don't buy about the Blues? Right there at the centre of the Blues is a hard luck story. 'I woke up this morning and my baby had gone.' Of course she'd gone. She'd gone to people who didn't see themselves as victims. She didn't want someone *singing* about injustice she wanted justice. My generation escaped from all that ignorance and self-pity. And then you guys show up and say: 'This is it, this is the holy truth of the black race.' Which is why there's no black people at your gigs. My father and his kind didn't shoot the white bosses. They shot each other. And next morning they sobered up and begged forgiveness from the Lord Jesus Christ.

KARL. The band's finished. Tomorrow is the final gig. They don't want to tour and they don't want to play the blues.

DELLA. The lone man on the road with his guitar –

KARL. Yeah. And I can't do the music on my own. I need a few dudes to hold the wire for me. And when I don't have the music – that's when I stare at the wall. And the demons come out. And next thing, I'm walking down the road to meet The Man who will put it all right with one golden shot.

DELLA. Well Karl, you've truly touched my heart, but I care more about him than I do about you and I care more for me than I do about either of you. So you go die in a gutter with your needles, I don't give a shit.

Pause.

KARL. I just want to talk to him. I know he won't do the gig. I want to ask him some stuff. The man is my hero, you understand.

DELLA *goes to* KARL, *runs her hand down his face a moment then breaks away.*

DELLA. He won't talk about the crossroads.

KARL. No?

DELLA. But if you like. I'll tell you the truth.

KARL. Yeah?

DELLA *lights cigarettes for them both.*

DELLA. A travelling musician was a vulnerable man. The law, jealous husbands, drunks. He needed some force on his side, build up a little mystique. Satan makes a neat bodyguard.

KARL. Doesn't explain how he learned to play.

DELLA. He disappeared. For a time. Something he got very good at later. But why?

KARL. Sometimes you have to make a quiet move. Blow on the dice before the next shake.

DELLA. You're seeing him moving *towards* something. Wasn't like that. He was running away.

KARL. A woman?

DELLA. No.

KARL. Another shooting?

DELLA. Ku Klux Klan. (*Pause.*) 1921 was a key year in their history. A time for targetting specific individuals. People who had turned their back on plantation labour, people who had made a statement or taken a stand. They'd trump up a rape charge and then you were a hunted animal.

KARL. This is the Black Studies programme.

DELLA. The story is he went away for three days. It's bullshit. He used to wander from town to town in the Delta, from

wife to wife, never settling. No one's gonna notice him
gone for three days. It would have to be longer, six months,
maybe a year. He was hiding from the Klan. If you were on
their list you were beyond hope. Lynching, castration. Some
black people were gouged to death with corkscrews. He was
holed up in a shack just outside the Delta on some waste
ground. Couldn't work, couldn't sing for money, couldn't
show his face. All he's got is his guitar. He's playing it
fifteen goddamn hours a day for six months, hungry as a
dog. When the heat's off, he comes back a changed man.
Of course people hear a difference when he plays. Nothing
to do with the Devil. It's called practice.

KARL. Doesn't make sense. He could've jumped a train, gone
North.

DELLA. The Klan was strong everywhere, a national
organisation. You couldn't run. You had to find a place to
hide.

Pause.

KARL. You know how you tell that story. You tell it from the
inside.

DELLA. I spent a lot of my life trying to get into that man's
head.

KARL. I don't mean that. I mean you tell it like it's your own
story.

DELLA (*beat*). Excuse me.

KARL. The fugitive trip. How come you play that number so
well? Is that practice? Or is it for real?

DELLA *stiffens.*

DELLA. Two things, Karl. One, I grew up with the man so
I know him from the inside. Two, I went away. So I got him
in perspective. Got him in a political context.

KARL. But then you came back again.

DELLA. So?

KARL. So if you just told your own story – which you did –
then who's your Klan? And why does someone who went

out and bought herself an expensive item like a perspective come back to live here in Two Bar Junction, Nowheresville?

DELLA. My father is an old man –

KARL. He needs nothing. You're here 'cos you need him.

JESSE *comes back in. He carries an old framed photograph.* DELLA *suddenly grabs a shawl from the stand by the door and slams out.*

JESSE *goes out onto the porch. He looks to the left, then to the right. He sees* DELLA.

JESSE. Della! (*Pause.*) Della!

JESSE *stands looking on the porch looking out for a few moments. Then he comes inside and shuts the door.*

JESSE. Turning cold. What she doin'?

KARL. I don't know, man. (*Beat.*) You gotta keep a grip on your womenfolk.

JESSE. Hell, I only just walked in. Look to yourself. You're the young cock with all the bucks in your pocket and you can't keep a woman in a room two minutes.

KARL. She's not my womenfolk.

JESSE. You wanna check your perfume, boy, you're givin' out the wrong odours.

KARL. I'm giving out nothing.

KARL *gets another whiskey glass.*

JESSE. You find my daughter attractive?

KARL. I came to see you.

JESSE. She not good enough for you?

KARL. She's cool.

JESSE. She give you politics? Black white politics?

KARL. I handled it.

JESSE. That's what she does, see. There ain't no malice in it, that's how she sees the world, black and white.

KARL. If that's her riff. Whiskey?

JESSE. No, I won't take no whiskey tonight.

KARL *pours himself a large one and takes a slug.*

JESSE. I don't want to show my daughter no disrespect, but I just don't go along with her. There's black, there's white, I see plenty bad in both.

KARL. Yeah?

JESSE. Hell, they talk against them plantation bossmen, but I had some high times with them fellers. Runnin' moonshine whiskey, cuttin' deals on the cotton. If you showed a little grit and cut it on their side against the laws, they would treat you right.

KARL. There was worse white guys than the plantation owners.

JESSE. Sure. There was the mission fathers.

KARL. There was the Klan.

JESSE. Ha! The Klan that weren't so much. People talk up the Klan, we did a lot of stuff pretendin' they was the Man when we wanted cover for somethin' else.

KARL. Yeah?

JESSE. Sure. There was a lot of bad things went down, that's for sure, but it ain't at all how it's painted. Della, she's read it, but she didn't live it and there's things that went down she likes to forget 'cuz they ain't too convenient. Niggers cheatin', robbin', shootin' each other.

KARL. Is that right?

JESSE. I ain't sayin' nothing 'gainst Della, mind. She come back to me, I never asked her. She come to be close to me. She had a good career at the university, teachin'. But she weren't happy. I don't have no congress with women no more. But I have her and I tell you this, the purest thing you will ever find is a man's love for his daughter. Beats any kind of love. It's a love of two spirits.

Suddenly JESSE *hands* KARL *the photograph.*

Now Karl. What you make of this?

Please fill in, stamp and return this card if you wish to be kept informed about new publications from Nick Hern Books

Name

Address

Post code

The most recent NHB catalogue I have is dated

Comments

Nick Hern Books
14 Larden Road
London
W3 7ST
UK

AFFIX
STAMP
HERE

KARL *looks at the photograph.*

KARL. Hey.

JESSE. He says 'Hey'.

KARL. Old photograph.

JESSE. Old, old photograph. Tell me what you see.

KARL. Never seen this. There's you.

JESSE. Uh-huh.

KARL. Blind Gary Davis.

JESSE. Tell me what you see.

KARL. This here is Son House.

JESSE. Well now.

KARL. This cat here . . . I don't know.

JESSE. Me and Gary and Son and Mr. No-name.

KARL. Maybe, I don't know, Clarence Brown. Must be nineteen forty, forty-one, maybe Chicago, outside some club.

JESSE. Not bad. Not bad. You got me and Gary and Son, and you got Chicago. Not forty or forty-one but it is forty-three. And Mr. Mystery ain't Clarence Brown.

KARL. Tommy McClennan?

JESSE *laughs at* KARL.

JESSE. See, you get it and you don't get it.

KARL. Tell me who it is.

JESSE. 'For he hath shut their eyes, that they cannot see; and their hearts, that they cannot understand.'

KARL *is a little riled by this routine but he hides it.*

KARL. Well, tell me.

JESSE *gives him a Cheshire cat grin.* KARL *ponders. He doesn't know whether to tackle this head on or let it lie. At length:*

KARL. You want me to show you something?

JESSE. O.K.

KARL. I brought my new guitar along.

JESSE. In the car?

KARL. Yeah.

JESSE. Doesn't that chauffeur of yours get bored?

KARL. It's advertised as a boring job. I could show it to you.

JESSE. You think I'd go for that?

KARL. It's a custom made Martin D-45. Exact replica of yours. I sent the spec out when I knew we were coming over. Picked it up in Pennsylvania last week. Played it onstage for your three numbers tonight.

JESSE. You know, I never did like guitars that much. Nice furniture, but they attract a contrary class of person.

KARL. It's a beautiful guitar.

JESSE. You can't go out and buy a guitar. Order one from some personality you never seen. It would be like walking into a store and asking if they can fit you up with a new soul. Your guitar has to come to you. You have to be patient. It will come. And when it does it will sing to you. That's how you play the blues. You sing and your guitar sings back to you.

KARL. So how did you get that one?

Pause. JESSE *looks at the guitar on the wall, then turns back to* KARL.

JESSE. The fourth man in the photograph is the Reverend Gary Newton. A great preacher and a great man of the spirit. He was the only man that ever taught me a thing. We're not standing outside no club, we're standing outside the 19th Church of the spirit on the South side. You looked at that picture, you saw four bluesmen. Wasn't four bluesmen, it was four preachers.

KARL. You were a preacher?

JESSE. There. Thought you knew the whole story.

KARL. I never heard that before.

JESSE. I set you a test and you failed. The important thing is not the music. The important thing is the spirit. That's how come I pretended to die. What I loved most in life had gone. I left life behind so my spirit could live.

KARL. So what you're saying is: There's a car crash, right, Angela, the greatest love of your whole life, your wife –

JESSE. Rest her soul –

KARL. She's killed. Outright. There's some confusion at the scene, there's another body in the car, cops assume it's you. And you're . . . what? . . . 'I'll go along with that.' You skip the funeral of the woman you love, so that you can just fade out.

JESSE. 'A little while and ye shall not see me; and again a little while and ye shall see me.'

KARL. And the one thing you can do. Which is sing the blues, which you do better than anyone else on the planet, all the other guys are dead, I mean really dead, right? The one thing you can do, you stop doing. These four walls and you're staring at them.

JESSE. You know, there's an art to wasting time. It's easy to make time pass. But to be conscious of wasting every second as you waste it, that takes a little skill.

KARL. I don't get it.

JESSE. I was a sinful man, I had sinned against the Lord.

KARL. I don't get it.

JESSE. Why should I tell you anything. I don't know nothin' about you. So where comes the right for you to know about me?

KARL. I'm like you. I'm a bluesman.

JESSE. You know, it interests me that this music which came from work, from hollers in fields should appeal to a bunch of people who never done a lick of work in their lives. Hell, they made themselves a job out of avoidin' work.

KARL. Well, Jesse, you all made work sound so scary. (*Pause.*) O.K. I'll tell you about me. I am different from you. I love guitars. I drool over them.

KARL *gets up. He fixes his eye on the guitar above the mantelpiece. He walks towards it.*

They're like girls to me, you know what I'm saying. They look so, so good. You can't keep your hands off. I can't be in a room with a guitar without touching it. Got to have it on my lap.

Pause.

But you've sat here in the same room as this beautiful guitar for fourteen years. And not a touch. I don't know how you could do that. So I was wondering. I was wondering, if you won't touch it. I was wondering if you would let me touch it.

Pause. KARL is now quite close to the guitar.

I'm right up by it, Jesse. I'm hard up to it. Will it be O.K. Will it be cool for me to take it down, for a touch?

Pause. KARL reaches towards the guitar.

JESSE. I always called that guitar Angela.

KARL is stopped in mid air.

KARL. This guitar?

JESSE. Yes sir, I called her Angela.

Pause.

KARL. She's beautiful.

JESSE. She always was a beauty.

Pause. KARL reaches up and takes the guitar down from the wall. JESSE doesn't turn round.

KARL. I've taken her down, man.

JESSE. I thought that you had.

KARL walks halfway back to the table. He plays a chord softly. It's way out of tune. JESSE doesn't react.

KARL. Fourteen years.

KARL walks back to the table with the guitar. He sits.

Mind if I tune her up?

JESSE stares at KARL, saying nothing.

Taken a battering over the years. Need a bit of work on this, get it back in shape.

KARL *tunes the guitar. JESSE watches impassively.*

I've got a great guy, Nick, guitar technician, top man in his field. He could work on it for you.

JESSE. You know guitars die if you don't play 'em.

KARL. It's true, but Nick resurrects them. Didn't have those guys back in your day, did you? Not even a roadie. We have an army now. People to do the hair, wardrobe. Status Quo, they have a Tequila roadie, dig that. That's the guy's job, look after the Tequilas. Mind you, lot of responsibility, frosting the glasses, salt, limes. Fresh limes when you're playing, I don't know, Budapest, could be a tight call. Big job. There you go.

And the guitar is in tune.

Feels a bit stiff, lot of dirt back of the strings. Action's a bit high. Is it O.K if I play? I thought I might sing you a tune. A Robert Johnson tune.

JESSE. You can play, man. You can sing. If you think you have the right.

Pause. KARL *plays a blues intro, then begins to sing, tentatively at first, then with increasing confidence.*

KARL.
Early this morning when you knocked upon my door
Early this morning when you knocked upon my door
And I said 'Hello, Satan, I believe it's time to go.'

Me and the Devil was walking side by side
Me and the Devil was walking side by side
I'm gonna beat my woman until I get satisfied

She say you don't see why that I will dog her round
She say you don't see why that I will dog her round
It must be that old evil spirit so deep down in the ground

You may bury my body down by the highway side
You may bury my body down by the highway side
So my old evil spirit can catch a greyhound bus and ride.

Long pause. Then JESSE *pours two whiskies.*

JESSE. You know, I think we should drink a toast. To Mr. Robert Johnson.

They drink.

I played a few times with Robert. But it weren't no good. He was a suspicious son of a bitch and when he got a crowd gathered he would say, 'Come on, Jesse, we'll stand and sing back to back, then if any shit goes down, at least one of us is gonna be ready.' He'd set you up like that, so that even if everything was peaceful, you'd start to get vexed, looking at old womens, wondering if they was packing a 44 in their washing baskets. Then, middle of a song he'd quit. He'd just stop playing, put his guitar under his arm and walk away. Me I didn't ever want to quit till I'd made me some dough. So I would play on, peeking over my shoulder, looking for the knife in the back. Finish the song, collect, follow him, the way he'd gone, but he'd just disappeared into thin air. You'd run into him, six weeks later and he wouldn't say a word 'bout it. You bring it up, he'd give you a look like you was crazy, like he'd never even met you before. You get that every now and again, you come up against a personality where the normal rules don't fit. You look 'em in the eye and there's that long gone stare that tells you all bets is off. (*Pause*.) I tell you somethin', man. I done you a great wrong. Because you can play the blues.

KARL. Thanks, man.

JESSE. That almost sounded like my Angela.

KARL. I could get my guys to work on her, sound just like she used to. You just gotta say the word.

JESSE. You know I lied to you yesterday. I've heard your records. It's a pretty good band, man.

KARL. Thanks.

JESSE. You need to get rid of that bass player.

KARL. I'm working on it.

JESSE. So I want you to tell me about it.

KARL. The band?

JESSE. The tour you just done. Two million people. What's it like?

KARL. Like?

JESSE. Where you been, what's the action?

KARL. We been everywhere. Here, Far East, Europe.

JESSE. Never been those places. Tell me 'bout it.

KARL. All of it?

JESSE. Yeah, I wanna hear 'bout all of it.

KARL. You sure?

JESSE. I'm sure.

KARL. Tokyo was first up. We were locked in a rubbish skip four hours to escape the fans. Honolulu, Manila. Hong Kong, scored with two of the Governor's personal staff. Auckland, Brisbane, Melbourne. Adelaide, a dog was thrown from my hotel window in mysterious circumstances. Dead on impact. So the Royal Randwick Racecourse, Sydney, is picketed by Animal Rights protesters and Andrew kicks off the first number in a different key from the rest of us. Singapore, David punches me in the kidneys just before we go back for the encore. I never mention it. Then Europe. Montreux. Stiff with minor royalty. Ever had a blue-blood blow-job? Great, beyond description. Small, dull riot at the Festhalle, Frankfurt. Then bigger, much more professional riots at Munster, Kiel, Bremen. Solid, German riots, tear gas, the works. Brussels lost all our luggage, went on with borrowed amps. Dortmund, David falls victim to a bout of food poisoning. Sad. Amsterdam, Ian tries to get busted for possession, gets fined for a litter offence. Les Abattoirs, Paris, we're crap, but then we're always crap in Paris and they never notice. On the plane to Scandinavia, Andrew learns a joke in Norwegian, tells it between numbers in Gothenburg only to find out that Gothenburg's in Sweden, gets hit by a bottle, mild concussion. Indoor rain at the Vejby Risskov Hallen in Aarhus, Denmark. Then Reykjavik and Oslo. No, I'm embarrassed to tell you about Oslo.

JESSE. Come on, how bad can it be?

KARL. Oslo, I didn't get laid.

JESSE. Didn't get laid. What happened?

KARL. It slipped my mind.

JESSE. Forgot to get laid!

KARL. I know, I know –

JESSE. Man, you done something there I never done.

KARL. Plaza de Toros Monumental, Barcelona, Terry fell off the stage –

JESSE. He the bass player?

KARL. Yeah. Thirty thousand feet of steel decking, his feet can't find it. Then the Americas. Ontario, Seattle, Buffalo, New York. The Cow Palace, San Francisco great, De Moines, awful. Vancouver one of the blow-up women drifts away from her moorings, Chicago, Indiana, Georgia. Thing with tours is that sometimes, for no reason, like it's not a great venue, the fans are nothing special, the sound check sucks, but for some reason you go out there and you cut it, it tops everything and you're flying. And that's what we did at the War Memorial Coliseum, Greensboro, North Carolina. I go offstage high as a kite. Backstage, suddenly the others are pushing all the hangers-on out of the room. They back me up against a wall and they say: 'This is it. This tour is the end. We've all decided. We want the country house, the wife, the kids, a different Greatest Hits album every other year and no more hassle.' And they march out. And there I am with my fear. Of being left on the road on my own with a guitar. And I lose it, man. I go straight out to find the Man and somewhere I lose a week of my life. Maryland and Dallas I'm told we go on, I don't remember. A doctor is called. There's a clinic in Mexico I did time there four years ago, it's *the* place, you understand. I wake up there, the no name hacienda: blood change, counselling, three days climbing walls. South America is cancelled. I'm told to go home. Everyone else wants to go home. I say: 'No, I will not go home.' For the last time, I lift those four passengers on my back and I carry them forward.

Jacksonville, Louisville, Hampton Virginia. A week in
Madison Square Gardens. Cleveland, Milwaukee. The Cobo
Hall, Detroit. Memphis. Baton Rouge you just heard. Then
the last gig. The last gig ever. New Orleans tomorrow.

Pause. KARL is very upset.

JESSE. Your geography gets pretty good.

KARL. Yes it does.

JESSE. Don't know how you recall all that shit.

KARL. There's a T-shirt. I'll get you one.

JESSE. You see why, from what you was just sayin', bout the
high old times on tour and all. You can see why they hate
us.

KARL. Who?

JESSE. Other men. We got it all. We go up on that stage – and
Karl, it don't make a difference if this is a big steel deck in
front of fifty-seven thousand people, or a one foot wooden
platform at the back end of a bar. The point is, we get to go
up there, on high. And we strut in front of the ladies. And
what do they do, they fall for us. 'Cuz we're high up and
struttin' and we're doin' the thing their men would like to
do, only they can't. And they put out for us, course they do.
And what do we go? We go: 'Yes please, ma'am.' 'Cuz we
feel so good, we ain't about to say no. And the hearts of all
the other men in the room is turned against us. They may
pretend it ain't that way. They may mooch over and go:
'Hey man, how you play that lick?' Or 'What type of strings
you usin' there?' Or a hundred other things. But they
despise us, 'cuz we got that power, we got the power bone
in the mojo bag, you understand what I'm saying?

KARL. I know, I know.

JESSE. But see Karl, the thing is this. They make sure they get
their revenge on you.

KARL. Yeah?

JESSE. Oh yeah. You never noticed that? You think maybe
there's stuff happens in your life and you think that's bad

luck or you brought it on yourself or something but that ain't so. All these guys that you upset – hell you don't have to do nothin' with their woman, they just got to *think* you done somethin' – they will store up trouble for you. They will make bad things rain down upon your head.

KARL. You're talkin' about my life, man.

JESSE. You know how they used to treat the musicians in Africa. I met a drummer from Nigeria down New Orleans one time. He was the best I ever heard and he told me from way back, they play it like this: while the musician is alive, he has everything, he has money, the pick of the womenfolk, everything he wants. Except they don't hold him in no regard: to his face, yes, behind his back, they talk him down and think him the lowest of the low. And when he comes to die, he don't get buried. That's how that works: they hold him so low in their esteem, he don't get a common burial. They take the body and they set it upright in a hollow tree and they leave it there to rot. Because they say the musician has had converse with the Devil. And that's what they do.

KARL. You can't let that stuff get to you.

JESSE. Oh, it gets to you. You play for long enough, it gets to you. That's why I should have stopped. (*Pause.*) Angela she told me. She said: 'You can't live your whole life. this way. Folks set their mind against you. You better quit.' But I wouldn't do it. I was stubborn, and it ain't even like I was pullin' big money, late nineteen fifties, I was doin' well to turn five dollars a week. I held on, makin' like the good times was just a little stretch away. But Angela, she saw the way it was goin', like the womens do, so she goes: 'Jesse, you go on the way you are now, but if you get to sixty years old and you're still up there playin' the blues for nickels and dimes, then I will leave you and I don't care what.' And I never paid it much mind, didn't matter how many times she said it, and she said it over and over, I just didn't pay no heed. Two months after I turned sixty she goes: 'Well, Jesse I told you plain and you ain't done a thing except carry on so I'm goin' off 'cuz I found a younger man and he ain't a musician so he don't get nightmares 'bout what's

stored up for him.' And the thing was, he sure wasn't no
musician, but he was a no good man, he was a drifter, didn't
have nothing, no family, no job, the sort of personality that
would come to your door and grind kitchen knives for a
dollar. So I'm thinkin' hell, she meant it all those years, but
now I'm sore 'cuz this young nobody done made off with
my woman and took my station wagon. I ain't even got the
transport to get to where I'm going. I'm all on my own
some rooming house in Illinois, I reads it in the paper. He
turned my wagon over, didn't know the steering, off a high
ledge into a big ravine, there she goes and they're two days
pickin' bits of flesh out of metal, bits of metal out of the
dust, the cops figure me for him, what do they care, a nigger
is a nigger, one's the same as another. And I'm on my own,
I'm grievin'. I start to head to Chicago, I know where she'll
be buried. I ain't got no money, no transport. I just got a
guitar, I'm sixty years old and I'm doin' what I did with
Robert when we was young, jump a train, hitch a ride on
a farm wagon, on the road, alone, your guitar in your hand.
No one knows me. I get to the entrance of the church yard.
They got a kind of archway there, a couple of cypress trees
bent over towards each other. I'm stopped there. On the
verge. I'm standin' there, five minutes, ten. And I find
myself walkin' away. I ain't goin' through with it. I don't
know what I'm thinkin'. Thing is, I ain't thinkin'. If I'm
thinkin' at all, I must be thinkin', my life is over. Ain't
nothin' will bring her back. What's better, the dignity of this
– you got killed with your wife, worst thing folks is gonna
say is his drivin' didn't get no cleverer. Or show up. And it's
your fault. A musician who can't keep his woman. A
musician whose wife will leave him for some hobo. If I was
thinkin' at all I thought that. But I just walked. Walked and
hitched rides all the way back down south. Took me the rest
of the year.

KARL. Back to the Delta.

JESSE. You come back to what you know. But it's a big old
place. I settled north of where I was raised, just like you
guessed. No one knew me. I got a job in a gas station. I
joined the Sanctified Church where they don't hold with no

blues. But mostly I just grieved. And I don't know if you've ever been in that position of grieving. You find yourself becoming the thing you're grieving over. Lying on a bed, motionless, jaw set, eyes staring. I only made one contact with the world. After a year I wrote to Della. Only child I had worth a damn. And she was so sore with me she wouldn't come at first. So I just kept myself in this room learnin' to be invisible.

KARL. You sung the blues then.

JESSE. Nope. If I had listened to Angel and quit them blues, she would be alive today. Took me ten years to admit that to myself. She done right. I lost her because I sang the Devil's music. And the Devil done took his dues.

KARL. Well you know, man, that's just one way of looking at it.

JESSE. Ain't no other.

KARL. Yeah, there's another. You took a fall, panicked and went back to what you were safe with. The real spirit was in the blues. The church was the drug that numbs the pain.

JESSE. The church is my strength.

KARL. I'm gonna test you out, man. I'm gonna sing you a blues and you won't resist it.

JESSE. Don't do that man. You played one of Robert's tunes already. It spooks me.

KARL. It spooks you 'cos you know it's the truth.

JESSE. Don't play no more blues man, it's bad luck.

KARL. I'm gonna play 'Churchyard Blues'.

JESSE. Don't play that tune, man.

KARL. It's your tune.

JESSE. I wrote that tune, but I don't want no part of it now.

KARL. You wrote that tune when you lost a woman.

JESSE. Angela. First time I lost her. I did her wrong and she come back.

KARL. She came back 'cos you sang for her, man.

JESSE. That ain't true.

KARL. You sang the blues so good, she heard your voice.
Heard it on a record and turned straight back to you.

JESSE. That's the legend.

KARL. But it's a true legend, yeah?

JESSE. There are some legends that happen to be the truth.
I guess that's one.

KARL. What I'm saying here, it wasn't hymn singing brought
her back.

JESSE. I should have sung church music for her –

KARL. Wouldn't have worked. She heard your voice on a
record player outside a grocery store, stopped in mid stride
and walked back to you.

JESSE. One thousand miles. Heard the song, hitched a ride,
caught a train, walked the rest – one thousand miles back to
me –

KARL. – because you sang her the blues

JESSE. Can't bring her back now –

KARL. – but you can make a visit. You can go to that place in
your mind where she is –

JESSE. I'm scared to go there –

KARL. That's why you go to church. Keep the fear strong. But
your soul isn't in the church, Jesse. Your soul's in the blues.

JESSE. The blues –

KARL. You wrote them. You were the man, you are the man –

JESSE. I wrote them blues like no one else 'cept Robert –

KARL. That's right. The two of you, the two of you –

JESSE. Me and Robert Johnson –

KARL. You know how this one goes –

JESSE. It won't bring her back –

KARL. You can go to the place where she is –

JESSE. I can go there, I can go there.

KARL. Let me take you, man, here's how it goes.

KARL starts to play a slow, slow blues. He sings, looking at JESSE all the time. JESSE's eyes are closed, his head tilted back, the front legs of his chair gradually lifting off the floor.

KARL. Believe I'm dead, lost my woman today
I believe I'm dead, I lost my woman today
Went down to the church but my heart's too sick to pray.

JESSE begins to sing.

If the Lord had mercy he'd have nailed her shoes by mine
If the Lord had mercy he'd have nailed her shoes by mine
But he stove my brain and took a hammer to my spine

Now JESSE stands, eyes still closed, singing loud, taking the song over from KARL.

My body's broke and my soul is damned to hell
Said my body's broke and my soul is damned to hell
That Devil Lord got me right down under his spell.

The door opens. DELLA hurtles in, the shawl wrapped round her head and shoulders. She stares at JESSE. KARL sees her and plays even louder. JESSE is at the height of his passion, singing from the depths of his soul.

Believe I'm dead, lost my woman today
I believe I'm dead, I lost my woman today
Went down to the church but my heart's too sick to pray.

KARL brings the song to an end. JESSE opens his eyes. He sees DELLA.

JESSE. You brought her back! You brought her back to me!

Quick blackout.

Interval.

ACT TWO

Scene One

Lights up. Late morning. The curtains are drawn but the door to the porch is open and warm sunlight streams in.

JESSE *sits on an old wooden chair on the porch, maybe snoozing, maybe staring into space. Some moments.*

DELLA *comes on through the connecting door. She carries two travelling bags and places them on the floor.*

DELLA. OK, Pop.

JESSE. Mmmnn?

DELLA. I said O.K.

    JESSE *gets up and wanders into the room. He stretches.*

JESSE. Nice day.

DELLA. Are you O.K. with this?

JESSE. We get into your car. We drive west.

DELLA. North.

JESSE. We drive north? We going Memphis?

DELLA. No, Pop, we're not going to Memphis. Too many people.

JESSE. Ain't nobody gonna recognise me in Memphis. First place everybody forgotten me, second place I don't look like me any more.

DELLA. People know me in Memphis. We're going St. Louis.

JESSE. Long way. Why we going there?

DELLA. Because it's a long way and no one knows us.

JESSE. I played a house party St. Louis 1938, might get recognised.

DELLA. We take that chance.

JESSE. Was a big old party. We gonna sleep in the car?

DELLA. We'll find somewhere.

JESSE. I ain't sleepin' in no car.

DELLA. We'll find somewhere.

JESSE. We get in the car. We drive St. Louis, we get there. It's dark?

DELLA. It'll be dark.

JESSE. We stay, we come back next day.

DELLA. No, we stay another day.

JESSE. We must like St. Louis. We stay another day. Then we come back.

DELLA. Yeah, then we come back.

JESSE. We sleep a second night same place –

DELLA. Maybe, maybe different place –

JESSE. Sleep a second night, drive back home.

DELLA. That's it. Two days, we're covered.

JESSE. He could come back after two days.

DELLA. Two days and it's the end of tour. The circus moves on.

JESSE. And we carry on like before.

DELLA. Just like before.

JESSE. And Karl won't tell no one, he won't bother us.

DELLA. I think he respects you that much.

JESSE. He's gonna be upset. That I ain't here.

DELLA. Pop, it'll be bad for you to go up on that stage. I worry for you. And I can't trust you once he walks through that door.

JESSE. Can we leave him a note?

DELLA. Don't be stupid, Pop.

JESSE. I like the guy. I wanna leave him a note.

Pause.

DELLA. O.K. Leave a note.

JESSE. Sayin' what?

DELLA. It's your note.

JESSE. Get me some paper.

DELLA *pulls a sheet of paper out of her notebook. She brings the paper and a pen over to the table.*

JESSE. Write it for me. Dear Karl.

DELLA (*writing*). Yuh?

Pause.

JESSE. I could not do it. To myself and my memories. I hope you understand.

DELLA *writes.*

DELLA. And maybe say: 'Don't contact me again.'

JESSE. 'Please don't contact me again. Enjoy our secret.' O.K.

DELLA *finishes the note. She stands.*

DELLA. O.K. You ready to go?

JESSE. No.

DELLA. Why not? He's gonna be here soon.

JESSE. Guy's a musician, he ain't gonna be here before noon. Said he'd stop by around two o'clock. That means half past four.

DELLA. I'm not taking chances, Pop. Come on.

JESSE. No.

DELLA. Why not?

JESSE. 'Cuz I ain't comin'.

Pause.

DELLA. Pop. We talked this through. I've just written you a note.

JESSE. I ain't comin'.

DELLA. Why not?

JESSE. I've thought about this, Della, and I hear you say how
if I play up there on that big steel stage it's gonna be bad for
me, for my religion, my peace and quiet. But I don't believe
you. You never cared for my religion, you always used to
say I should trade my peace for the royalties I'm owed.
So I don't know. I think you got some other reason for
runnin' off. And the upshot is: I ain't movin' till you tell
me what it is.

DELLA. I don't agree with your religion, Pop, but it sustains
you. Once the people in that church know you played the
Devil's music, they won't take you back.

JESSE. I don't want to hear this shit. This ain't what you think
and it never has been.

DELLA. That Karl is no good for you. I'm gone fifteen
minutes last night, he's got you singing the blues and
thinking I was *her* –

JESSE. Way you wore that shawl made you look like my
Angel, that's all it was –

DELLA. He had you thinking Momma was back from the
dead –

JESSE. Well I don't think that now. I took too much whiskey,
got heated up. I'm cooled down now, I hear you defendin'
my religion and I gets suspicious. Don't matter how much
pretty paper you wrap around skunk meat, folks don't
wanna buy it.

DELLA *goes to her shoulder bag. She lights up a cigarette.
She goes to the door, looks out at the porch. Then she shuts
the door. The room darkens. She turns back into the room
and sits down opposite* JESSE.

DELLA. O.K. You want it, you get it. Pop, I'm in trouble.

JESSE. You think I don't know that. You come to me six
months back, I knew then you were in trouble. I just gave
thanks to the Lord that in such a time I was there to help
you.

DELLA. A guy got shot. A white guy. I didn't shoot him. But
the gun he was shot with is registered to me. That's it.

JESSE. Guy got shot dead.

DELLA. Yeah, he's dead.

JESSE. Six months back.

DELLA. Yeah.

JESSE. With your gun. Why d'you have a gun?

DELLA. I'm an American and I need to protect myself.

JESSE. What kind of gun?

DELLA. Forty-five.

JESSE. And you lend this forty-five. To a friend?

DELLA. Yeah.

JESSE. A guy.

DELLA. Yeah.

JESSE. A lover man?

DELLA. What does that matter?

JESSE. The guy is your lover man, right?

DELLA. No, he ain't.

JESSE. Just a friend.

DELLA. Not really.

JESSE. A political friend.

DELLA. A brother, yeah.

JESSE. And the dead guy, who happens to be white is not a
   political friend, he would be more like a political opponent.

DELLA. A judge.

   Pause.

JESSE. Dead guy is a judge.

DELLA. He sentenced a group known as the Baltimore Three.
   They are serving a total of eight life sentences for crimes
   which they did not commit. A decision was made within the
   movement that Judge Hanlan should be executed by a group
   with no connection to the case.

JESSE. Which is where your 'friend' walks in.

DELLA. Correct.

JESSE. Only he can't use his own firearm, he has to borrow yours.

DELLA. A decision was made.

JESSE. Judge is murdered in cold blood, right.

DELLA. Same way he sentenced.

JESSE. And your 'friend' the killer –

DELLA. His name is Joshua –

JESSE. They got him?

DELLA. Yes they did. They picked him up at a roadblock north of Baltimore thirty minutes after the killing. Joshua is doing thirty-five to life in Soledad. I been on the run ever since.

JESSE *goes to the sideboard, pours a good slug of Bourbon and knocks it back.*

JESSE. What did I do when I was twenty-seven?

DELLA. All right, Pop.

JESSE. What did I do?

DELLA. You served five years in Parchman for a firearms offence.

JESSE. That's what I did.

DELLA. There was a difference.

JESSE. Do we learn nothing?

DELLA. There was a difference.

JESSE. What's the difference?

DELLA. The guy you shot was black.

JESSE. I kill a black guy. You help to kill a white guy. This is progress.

DELLA. That's right, Pop. One generation. Pretty fast, huh?

JESSE. Shouldn't have no gun. Black folks get enough trouble without bein' around firearms.

DELLA. What you want? I sit on the sidewalk singing 'We Shall Overcome.'

JESSE. Hold on here.

DELLA. We shall overcome *some* day, not *now*.

JESSE. Hold on here a minute.

DELLA. It isn't even a good tune.

JESSE. You're sayin' . . . what you're sayin' here . . . is the reason you come back to live with me . . .

DELLA. No, it's not that –

JESSE. The reason you come back to live with me. Is because I'm dead –

DELLA. – it's not what you're thinking –

JESSE. The Feds look at it, they think 'Where's she gonna go? What about her folks?'

DELLA. Don't, Pop.

JESSE. 'Nope. Cold trail. Here's the records. Died together in their automobile, 1961. She sure ain't gonna hole up there.'

DELLA. Yeah.

JESSE. Ain't that the truth?

Pause.

DELLA. Yeah.

JESSE. It's perfect. Other side of the country. Stayin' in a sleepy place where no one knows you with a man who's dead.

DELLA. Pop, we were always close.

JESSE. We never been this close. Not till this last six months. Now I know why.

DELLA. O.K. I admit that's why I came. But it didn't work out like I thought. We've got so close.

JESSE. But if I go up on that stage, the world's gonna beat a path here. Including the Feds. How close are we then?

DELLA. I only need a little more time, Pop. Then I can break cover under a different name.

JESSE. Is that what the brothers are telling you? Bullshit.

DELLA. Please, Poppa. Karl will persuade you. We run now, he goes home, we're safe.

JESSE sits. He seems suddenly beaten.

JESSE. All I hear from you is 'run.'

DELLA. It would have been O.K. if he hadn't come.

JESSE. But he did come. The guy who can turn the whole shebang upside down always does come.

DELLA. Yes. He does.

JESSE. See, people chastise me all my life for singin' 'bout but one thing. How women betray me. The Devil enters a woman, makes her betray me. They say 'Don't sing that stuff, Jesse, it ain't true.' But I tell you one thing. That's all I ever knowed.

Knocking at the door. DELLA and JESSE exchange glances.

JESSE. Get that.

DELLA. If it's him –

JESSE. Then it's him. Get it.

JESSE turns his chair with the back towards the door and composes himself. DELLA sees the travelling bags and drags them off through the connecting door. A louder knock. DELLA comes back and opens the door.

KARL is standing there. He's dressed from head to foot in black. He carries a black guitar case and a black hold-all. Under one arm he holds a black attaché case.

KARL. Hi Della.

DELLA. Hi.

KARL. You O.K.?

DELLA walks away and sits down, leaving the door slightly ajar. KARL kicks it wide open. He stands in the threshold. No one's looking at him. He puts everything down. He stands, waiting. Eventually:

KARL. Hi, Jesse.

JESSE. You back again?

KARL. I said I would come back again.

JESSE. You are a most persistent type of personality.

KARL. I made an arrangement with you.

JESSE. Yeah. Not this early.

Pause.

KARL. It's kind of a slow day here.

JESSE. It just ain't our chatterin' time.

KARL. Right. Jesse. How you doin'?

JESSE. I'm doin' just fine.

Pause. KARL *sits down. He lights a cigarette.*

KARL. I went to this clinic once. You're sitting in a room, day one, the Doc walks in and says: 'How are you?' You go: 'I'm fine, I'm fine.' He goes: 'You are in a clinic for drug addiction. What do you have to feel fine about?' and walks out again. And then, man, then it gets to you. The next day you don't say 'I'm fine' and you don't let him walk out. You keep him there till you've fallen apart in front of his eyes. Just so there's no misunderstandings.

JESSE. Well. I'm still fine.

DELLA. And I'm fine too.

KARL. Well, great.

DELLA. We are God's own happy little rabbits here.

KARL. Well, I'll just wait.

Silence. KARL *waits.* DELLA *and* JESSE *ignore him. At length:*

JESSE. Karl?

KARL. It works.

JESSE. Say, Karl –

KARL. It works even if you don't leave the room.

JESSE. You know. What we talked about yesterday. I'm
   wondering if that would be such a smart thing to do.

KARL. Smart?

JESSE. Yeah. That's what I was wonderin'.

KARL. Look out the window, man.

JESSE. Why do I wanna look out the window?

KARL. Just do it, man.

   JESSE *gets out of his chair and walks to the window. He
   pulls back the curtain.* KARL *doesn't look at him.*

KARL. What you see?

JESSE. I see the church.

KARL. Look the other way. Down the street.

   JESSE *looks. He smiles briefly. Lets the curtain fall.*

JESSE. What is that exactly?

KARL. It's a Cadillac, Jesse. It's the Cadillac you're going to
   ride in today.

JESSE. Yeah, I saw them fins and I thought it was most likely
   a Cadillac.

KARL. It's a 1959 Cadillac Eldorado Biarritz. They only made
   thirteen hundred. With my own eyes I saw Keith Moon
   write off three of them, so they're can't be too many left.

   JESSE *holds back the curtain and stares at the Cadillac.*

   We can take it real slow so you can enjoy the comfort. Or
   we can take it real fast so you appreciate the power.

JESSE. That's one long automobile.

KARL. Nineteen feet.

JESSE. Nineteen feet. I lived in smaller places than that. Hell,
   I played in smaller places than that. Della, come look at this
   thing.

DELLA. I'm O.K. here, Pop.

JESSE. I never rode in no Cadillac.

KARL. We got a choice, Jesse. That's why I came early. We can take it all the way to New Orleans. Or we can take it for a spin half an hour down the road and pick up the helicopter. Fly over the Delta. If you fancy it. It's up to you.

JESSE. I never flown, Karl.

KARL. No?

JESSE. Never been in no plane, never been in no helicopter.

KARL. It's absolutely up to you.

JESSE. I don't know if I would like that.

KARL. It's your gig. It's your call.

JESSE. Yeah.

JESSE *returns to his chair and sits down.*

KARL. You O.K., Jesse?

JESSE. Hell, Karl. I don't know 'bout this.

KARL. It's cool, Jesse. We'll play it any way you want to play it.

JESSE. I don't know if I can still get up and strut my stuff. All those people.

KARL. Listen, Jesse. We'll play it this way. We travel in the Cadillac. Or the chopper, whatever. We hit the stadium. It's cool. We don't say who you are, we keep you out the way. We got a trailer, you can take a nap, hang out, whatever. You can watch the show from the side of the stage. Just watch. You don't have to come on. But at the end, if you want to come on, you can come on. We can introduce you. Or not. You can sing or not sing, play or not play. It's all your call.

JESSE. 'And all the congregation worshipped and the singers sang and the trumpets sounded – '

KARL. Look at it like it's a day out.

JESSE. A day out.

KARL. You O.K. Jesse. You wanna take a drink?

JESSE. No. I won't take a drink just now.

KARL *goes back to the door and picks up the attaché case. He sets the case down on the floor by* JESSE.

KARL. Of course if you did play with the band, Jesse, you'd get your fee.

JESSE. Oh yeah? I thought it was like, we would just be jammin'. Just for the kick.

KARL. This isn't some hick set-up. You show, play with the band, a three number encore, we're fronting you for that, man.

JESSE. Well. That would be nice.

KARL *springs the lock on the case.* JESSE *stares at the money.*

KARL. Five g's.

JESSE. Is that five g's?

KARL. That's five thousand dollars.

JESSE. Hey.

KARL. We ain't gonna bring in a great pro and not front him for the gig, man.

JESSE. No, no.

KARL. If it's not enough, say. I just pulled a number out of the air.

JESSE. Looks like my price went up.

KARL. Changing times.

JESSE. Being dead is a smart career move.

KARL. Jim and Jimi did well. Brian, no.

KARL *draws up a chair and sits close to* JESSE.

KARL. You know, Jesse. When you and I played last night, it was just rough, off the top of our heads, but, no question, we cut it together. Let's look at this. My band, end of the tour, natural break, time to do some new stuff, you understand what I'm saying –

JESSE. Sure.

KARL. Who knows? The thing is this, I'm looking at a blank diary. We could turn each other on to some things.

JESSE. Right.

KARL. Get together. Two guitars, old blues classics, some new tunes. A little tour. Europe. Nothing heavy, you understand. Just a coupla mates gigging, right?

JESSE. Europe.

KARL. Or here. Whatever you fancy. Get away from this stadium shit, play some little clubs. An acoustic album. No sweat. Lay it down in a weekend. All the publicity, you re release your old material. Clean up the sound, put it out on our label. Bingo.

JESSE. I see what you're sayin'.

KARL. It's up to you is what I'm saying. I'm just sketching out some options here.

JESSE. This all means a lot to you, don't it?

KARL. Yes, Jesse, it does.

JESSE. I don't want to be a disappointment to you.

KARL. You'll never disappoint me.

JESSE. Maybe I won't be able to do it any more. I'll sound rusty.

KARL. No you won't, Jesse. I've taken care of that.

KARL *gets up. He walks over to the guitar case and carries it to* JESSE.

Here you are, Jesse. I had two guys working on it all night and all morning.

JESSE. Is this my Angela?

KARL *flips the case open.*

KARL. That's your Angela.

JESSE *stares at the guitar, his face impassive.*

JESSE. She's beautiful.

KARL. New strings. Rebuilt the damaged section at the back. Adjusted the action. Re-decorated the headstock. Coat of polish. Played her a little.

JESSE. Guitars die if you don't play 'em.

KARL. And they come back to life if you do.

DELLA *stands, looking at* JESSE *and the guitar.*

JESSE. She's beautiful.

KARL. Get her out, man.

JESSE. I don't know.

KARL. You should get her out.

JESSE. You think so?

KARL. Do it.

JESSE *stares at the guitar in its case on the floor. He stares for the longest possible time.* KARL *and* DELLA *stare at* JESSE. *Then* JESSE *reaches forward, removes the guitar from the case and rests it easily on one knee. Very slowly he plays an E major chord. He lets the sound resonate. It's glorious. He listens attentively as the last harmonics die away. He sits for some moments. Then he replaces the guitar lovingly in the case. Pause.*

JESSE. You brought her back to me.

KARL. O.K.?

JESSE. You brought her back to me.

JESSE *stands.*

JESSE. When do we go?

DELLA. Pop –

KARL. You need to change, Jesse. They don't want to see you like that.

JESSE. Hell, I'm wearing my best.

DELLA. Pop you're not going to do this.

KARL *hands* JESSE *the black hold-all.*

KARL. New suit. New shirt, shoes. Choice of three different ties. The hat you got.

JESSE. Everything's laid on, huh.

KARL. When you get on our bus, every worry is removed. Take the gear and get dressed.

JESSE. Right now?

KARL. Right now. Then we can take our time, enjoy the ride.

JESSE. I'm on my way. You know, maybe you were right. Maybe I didn't have the blues, that's why I ain't been playin'. I had somethin' but it weren't the blues.

JESSE takes the case and goes through the connecting door. Almost immediately, KARL slumps into the nearest chair as if suddenly drained of physical energy.

DELLA launches herself at KARL, flailing at his body.

DELLA. Fuck you. Fuck you.

They struggle. KARL throws her off.

KARL. Easy, easy.

DELLA. I couldn't stop you.

KARL. Take it easy.

DELLA. I knew what you were doing and I couldn't stop you.

DELLA is poised to attack him again.

KARL. Does he know what you're hiding from?

Pause. DELLA backs off.

DELLA. I told him just now.

KARL. Right.

DELLA. Because of you, he knows.

KARL. He was the safe house and he didn't know.

DELLA. That's why he's doing the gig.

KARL. I don't think so.

DELLA. I hurt him. He's doing it to hurt me back.

KARL. I don't think so. If I got him, I got him with the guitar.

DELLA. You've put my life in danger.

KARL. Well I don't know the story, so I can't rule on that one.

But I'd say if you live the outlaw life, you gotta live it. There's no place called home.

DELLA. Please. Don't let him play.

KARL. I have a choice in my life. Music or drugs. The music's winning. But the band's always dragged me down. To be seen with Jesse. To be the man who brings back The Man. People will go: 'Oh, right that's who Karl is. He's the real thing. He's not one of those plastic copies.' To me, Jesse is the music. If I've got Jesse, I've got the music and I can kick the drugs.

DELLA. It puts me on the run.

KARL. You do your shit, you take the rap. That's what I believe.

DELLA. Forget me. The thing I want for him is this. He's old. He's frail. He's spent fourteen years talking to nobody.

KARL. That's one tough guy.

DELLA. He's old. I want you to look after him.

KARL. He'll get the best.

DELLA. And I want him back here after.

KARL. He'll want to hang out –

DELLA. No.

KARL. O.K.

DELLA. I'll be here.

KARL. Thought you might be long gone.

DELLA. I need to know he's all right.

KARL. You're in trouble, you should run.

DELLA. I'll be here.

The connecting door opens. JESSE comes in. Shades. Gorgeous, colourful shirt. Wide tie with outrageous palm tree motif. Braces, trousers, matching socks, two-tone shoes. He carries the jacket over his shoulder, Sinatra style. He looks like the most venerable and sleekest shark in the ocean.

JESSE. So whadd'ya think?

KARL. Hey, Jesse. I mean. I'm not gonna get laid tonight. The competition is too stiff.

JESSE. Quit foolin'.

KARL. You're gonna need your own trailer.

JESSE. Della. I want you to come with me.

DELLA. Pop, I'm not comin'.

JESSE. I'm askin' you.

DELLA. I can't, Pop and you know why.

JESSE. You know, Karl. I'll maybe just watch.

KARL. Whatever.

JESSE. Old dog havin' a look at how the young dogs make out.

KARL. You'll have the best view in the house.

JESSE. I ain't decided.

KARL. That's cool.

JESSE. Long as it's understood.

KARL. Here let me help you with the jacket.

JESSE. Thanks, man.

    KARL *helps him into the jacket.*

KARL. Looking good.

JESSE. Check those lapels.

KARL. It's cool, the look is cool.

JESSE. Feels cool.

KARL. Jesse. You got the hat?

JESSE. Yeah. I kept the hat.

KARL. Good.

JESSE. The only thing I kept in shape was the hat.

    JESSE *goes to the peg and picks off the hat.*

KARL. The hat is a trademark.

JESSE. There.

KARL. The trademark hat, the famous axe.

JESSE picks up his guitar case.

JESSE. The trademark hat, the famous axe.

KARL. Are you ready?

JESSE puts the hat on. The finished article ready for the road.

JESSE. I'm ready.

Quick blackout.

Scene Two

Blackout. The New Orleans audience.

KARL (*voice-over*). Now cool it, 'cos I'm gonna make a presentation to you. Special guest for the encore. A man who taught me the blues over the miles, over the years. You know rock 'n' roll has its share of tragedies.

The crowd is hushed.

But sometimes the dead come back. Ladies and gentlemen, will you put your hands together for the return of Jesse 'The Man' Davidson.

The crowd exults.

Sound fades. Lights up on the living room. It's night. The door to the porch is open. One of the travelling bags is on the floor. DELLA sits smoking, a towel wrapped round her head. She walks out onto the porch, looks around, stubs out the cigarette, comes back.

She goes to the fridge, takes out a bowl of leftover rice. Sits and eats with a fork. She takes a mouthful. Puts down the fork, pushes the bowl away. Goes to the radio, punches a button, gets a brief blast of Carole King, switches off. Finally sits, doing nothing. Lights another cigarette. Waits.

A car approaches. It's the Cadillac. DELLA *stands. She goes over to the porch and looks out. She looks for a few moments then throws the cigarette into the street. She comes back into the room. She hovers, unable to decide whether to stay in the room or go. Looks towards the door, suddenly scurries to the connecting door. She stands, holding the door frame, just out of the room.*

KARL *comes in carrying the guitar. Immediately he turns back.*

KARL. All right, Jesse?

JESSE *comes in to view. Suddenly he stumbles, his legs giving way.* KARL *rushes to support him.*

Jesse, I got you.

JESSE. I'm O.K.

KARL. Let's get you in.

DELLA. Poppa!

JESSE. I'm O.K. I feel a little cold.

KARL. Take it easy, man.

DELLA. What you done to him?

KARL. Sit down, Jesse.

DELLA. I'll get a blanket. I told you this thing was no good.

JESSE *sits.* DELLA *exits through the connecting door.*

KARL. We'll have a drink. Let's have a drink.

JESSE. Just get my breath.

KARL. Are you O.K.?

JESSE. I'm O.K.

KARL *pours two stiff bourbons.*

JESSE. Got hit by a big wave back there.

KARL. Drink this Jesse.

JESSE. Got twenty years in me yet, see if I ain't.

KARL. Sip that bourbon, you'll feel good.

JESSE *takes a hit of bourbon. It visibly settles him.*

JESSE. Well. What I just done back there?

KARL. You done great, Jesse.

DELLA *comes back with a blanket.*

JESSE. Della. You know what I just done?

DELLA. Poppa, did you play the gig?

JESSE. I done took a ride in a helicopter. Was the most
beautiful thing.

DELLA *puts the blanket round* JESSE*'s shoulders.*

DELLA. Is that all you done, Pop?

JESSE. Don't fuss me.

DELLA. Poppa, you're cold.

JESSE. Goin' up in that thing. Noise of them big old blades
takes some believin'. Then you look down, you see the
Delta spread out under you. I saw the whole of my life in
them lights down below. Where I was born, cotton fields I
worked, places I done stuff. Looked down and saw this
cross roads. Landed just top of the ridge.

KARL. The chopper's cool. You got your freedom.

DELLA. Poppa. Forget the ride. Did you do it?

JESSE. We drove all the way down New Orleans in that big
old Cadillac. Man it was so fast and smooth, like we was
swallowing the road.

KARL. Swallow it whole.

JESSE. Thousands of folks around the stadium. It ain't even
time to go in for four hours.

DELLA. Just tell me, Poppa.

JESSE. Karl, he don't let on. He say, this here is Mr. D. He's a
friend of mine, just call him Mr. D. And we stand out on
that big old stage, it's all empty and they got thirty, forty
guys runnin' around getting the equipment ready, the big
amplifiers and the lights and all. And they all going 'How
you goin', Mr. D.?' 'Anything we can do for you, Mr. D.?'

Had a chicken leg cooked in hot chilli and a nice cool beer. I felt as good as I felt for a dozen years.

KARL. And they're all going like: 'Who's the dude, who's the dude?' 'Cos Jesse looks so great. And I just go: 'The dude helped me, long time ago.' And they go: 'But who is he?' I go: 'The dude is the dude, let's leave it at that.'

JESSE. And the crowd, they all start to come in, they're all screamin', chantin', hollerin'. White folks. I ain't never heard white folks put up such a revel as that. I'm thinkin': 'They finally got it. These are white people havin' a good time. Took 'em a hundred years but they got it.'

KARL. Everyone knows it's the end of the tour, and something colossal is gonna go down.

JESSE. And then Karl and the boys come on. I ain't ever heard such a sound. I thought Muddy was loud when he started playin' that electric thing he done, but *this*. I put my hands over my ears, it's still way too loud. Karl, my ears is ringin' still.

KARL. Nothing to worry about.

JESSE. You sure?

KARL. After four years, your ears stop ringing, then you do have something to worry about.

JESSE. And I do admit, I'm havin' a hard time. But slowly, I take my hands off of my ears and it don't seem so loud. That bass go through you, and the big drums but after a while it ain't so hard to stand and listen. And, Della, I told you, they play good.

KARL. We were better in Baton Rouge.

JESSE. See, they took what we done and they took it down a different road. Same music, just further down another road. It don't stand still 'cuz it can't stand still.

KARL. Then the time comes.

JESSE. The time comes. They play the last number and they go off. Only everybody knows it ain't the last number and they's gonna come back on again. I never did figure that, but that's the way she goes.

KARL. I announce him. Slowly he walks on. And there's maybe ten thousand people in tears –

JESSE. It's right, I walk on, there's a white boy twenty years old at the front and he's cryin'. Ain't sayin' nothin', just standin' with the tears streamin' down –

KARL. And I'm thinking we'll have to carry Jesse into this, fourteen years long time, let's look after the Man. But no. He counts us in, Shotgun Blues and it's fast, faster than we ever played it but on the beat, on the money. Usually I drive the band, the drums follow me and everyone else follows the drums. So even when we're good we're never quite in sync, but it works. From the off, Jesse sets the tempo and there's no question he is the Man. He's lead guitar AND he's the bassman AND he's the drummer. It's like all five of us are locked into his riffs. Just that acoustic patched into our system and it's all going through him, like there's a crash on the hi-hat but it seems to be coming out of his axe. There's a semi-tone run in the bass but I'm reading it off of his fretboard. And that's only the guitar. The voice is playing off that solid riff, just ahead of the beat, just behind the beat, playing with it, teasing it. He leaves one line so late you think he's not gonna make it, then he drifts it in so fast and sweet, a moment to smile at himself and back in time for tea; then the next line he's way ahead, puts the brakes on and it's like he just brought a stallion from a gallop to a halt in a second, and the last line he just sings it, so simple, so on the beat it's a revelation and the whole song lights up in your mind and we finish, and he steps back a little off the mike, wipes the sweat away and goes: 'Come on, let's hit the next one.'

JESSE. Yes sir, hit that snuff dippin' key –

KARL. And he hits it and I'm in heaven. The kids are blown away. The fuckin' crew are standing with their jaws hanging open, and we are someplace else. We are some place else. I don't know where we are man, but it isn't Planet Earth. And he stands there at the end, a sea of cigarette lighters and waving arms. And he touches the brim of his hat, goes: 'It's been a pleasure' and walks off. I thought I knew cool man. I thought I knew cool. I never knew cool till that moment.

DELLA. Was that what happened Poppa?

JESSE. Yeah. That's what happened. The old dog came out into the sun. And he showed the young dogs some tricks. He sure showed 'em.

DELLA. So. You're not dead any more.

JESSE. No. I ain't dead no more.

Suddenly there's a thud against the side of the house – a heavy object being thrown. JESSE stands. Then two more thuds close together. JESSE goes out onto the porch.

JESSE. What gives out here?

DELLA follows protectively, watching from the doorway. KARL sits drinking, still lost in his high.

DELLA. Poppa don't go out.

JESSE. Leave me be, child.

DELLA. You weren't so good just now, Pop.

JESSE. I'm O.K. Get back inside.

DELLA. Poppa, it's cold.

KARL. Leave him alone.

DELLA turns back into the room.

DELLA. Excuse me?

KARL. Why don't you leave Jesse alone and tell me the story.

DELLA. What story?

KARL. Babe, I look at you these three days, I see one thing. A woman on the run. How many things can a woman run from?

Pause.

You're not the type who runs from men. (*Pause.*) So it's something criminal. A robbery? Not your scene. An accidental killing. Maybe. Or something political.

DELLA. Quit jerking yourself off.

KARL. Some sort of protest. A bomb? Intellectuals are very fond of the home made bomb aren't they? An arson attack, a kidnapping that went badly wrong. Or badly right.

DELLA. Fuck you.

> KARL *stands and advances on* DELLA. *She backs off.*

KARL. I'm close, aren't I?

> KARL *backs* DELLA *against the wall.*

DELLA. Get out of my face.

> KARL *whips out an arm and pulls the towel away.*
> DELLA*'s head is shaved bald. Pause.*

KARL. So it's getaway time.

> *Pause.*

DELLA. Yeah. Because of you, it's getaway time.

> *A pause, then* DELLA *collapses on to him. He holds her for
> several moments.*

KARL. Here. Take it easy.

> KARL *sits her down and pours her a drink. She sips. They
> sit close together.*

DELLA. I've done six months here, face to the wall indoors,
face to the ground outdoors. I was almost in the clear.

KARL. I'm listening.

> *Pause.*

DELLA. I did stuff, good stuff. For young black kids.
Consciousness raising, education, making them feel they
had some power. Within the organisation I was trusted as a
woman and an intellectual, which means not trusted at all.
Everything had gotten bureaucratic, a parody of how we
started. Decisions were handed down from on high.
Grassroots activity was stamped out. I thought about
quitting but I knew that's what the guys at the top wanted.
So I made it known that I wanted to get involved in
something serious. The word came down that we had a
target, a judge. I have to show up with a gun in my shoulder
bag, wait for a guy called Joshua, hand it over, wait some
more and take it away afterwards. So the killer couldn't be
linked to the gun and the gun couldn't be linked to the
killer. I showed up – an underground lot where this judge
parks every Tuesday evening to see his mistress. And there's

Joshua, suit, tie, white shirt, guy looks like he's selling
insurance. He barks at me, takes the gun and says: 'Follow
me.' I go: 'No, the plan is I wait here.' He goes: 'Don't tell
me what the plan is, pussy.' So he's walking fast and I'm
running to keep up. And he goes: 'You watch me do this
one, you take the gun and you do the next one tonight.'
Suddenly there's two targets, the judge and another mark.
I'm going: 'What? You pull this stunt now and I go in with
the cops on red alert?' He says: 'This is how we test
people.' He's almost running now, I'm out of breath. There's
no build up. One second this white guy is getting out of a
blue Buick, the next Joshua is charging him, one shot puts
him on the floor, then in close – mouth, neck, stomach five
shots. Joshua drops the gun in my shoulder bag and a car
scoops him up. (*Pause.*) I stare at the dead guy. A long time.
I won't say I panicked, it didn't hit me that way. But what
I did was, I emptied the gun out of the shoulder bag and
walked. And I'm in freefall. The cops get lucky, pull Joshua
in at a roadblock, he hasn't made six miles.

KARL. Guy's in the can.

DELLA. He's in the can and the Feds and the brothers are on
my tail.

Pause.

KARL. I can help you.

DELLA. You people.

KARL. I'm gonna take Jesse back to England. Europe.

DELLA. You think so?

KARL. We have people who can fix things. You fly back as
part of the entourage. You're a backing singer.

DELLA. Don't you get it, Karl? I can't be with him. When he
was dead, the safest place in the world for me was with
him. Now you brought him back, he's where everyone will
go looking. You separated us for good.

Pause.

KARL. O.K. Let's look at it differently. The heat will be on.
I have to get you out now. You can take the chopper. There's

a place in Mexico. Very exclusive, very secure – a compound with barbed wire and dogs.

DELLA. What place?

KARL. My clinic. I'll fly you there, I'll front you. In three months, the heat will be off. What do you say?

DELLA. You people. You drop us in it so you can look good when you pull us out.

JESSE *comes in, walking slowly. He seems very tired.*

JESSE. Well then.

DELLA. What gives, Pop?

JESSE. Well, you know, it weren't nothin'.

JESSE *sits down.*

DELLA. Nothin'? What hit the side of the house?

JESSE. That was just some hothead boy.

DELLA. What boy?

JESSE. Alice's youngest.

DELLA. Gabriel?

JESSE. Hefted a piece of turf at the house.

DELLA. Three pieces.

JESSE. Yeah. (*Beat.*) Oh, Della, he saw me on the television. He saw me singing the blues at some friend's house, he's back faster than a rabbit, waking his Ma and she's straight out telling her friends. They won't allow me back in the church. First 'cuz I sang the Devil's music, second 'cuz I made out I was dead. I'm not welcome in the congregation. I won't even be welcome in this town.

DELLA. Poppa, come sit down.

JESSE. They say they're gonna hold a vigil right now, so I won't get no rest.

DELLA. Poppa.

JESSE. Karl, did I do you a favour today?

KARL. Yes, you did, Jesse.

JESSE. I'm real tired. Could you go out there and tell those people to go to bed and quit persecutin' an old man?

Pause.

KARL. Yes, Jesse, I can do that.

JESSE. I would be most grateful.

KARL *takes a hit of Bourbon then goes.* JESSE *follows him out onto the porch, watches. Then comes back.*

JESSE. What you done to your head, girl?

Pause.

You're goin' on the run.

Pause.

DELLA. Poppa, I let you down.

JESSE. Yes you did.

DELLA. I let you down bad.

JESSE. I ain't denying it.

DELLA. I let you down *twice.*

JESSE. That's right.

DELLA. The thing with the judge.

JESSE. Don't own a gun. And if you do, don't let no one else get hold of it.

DELLA. Then not telling you why I was here.

JESSE. I believed I was past hurtin' but that hurt.

DELLA. I know it did. I thought I was unhappy these last six months. But I see it now. I got close to you. I forgave you for pulling that dead man stunt.

JESSE. Yeah?

DELLA. I found some love for you.

JESSE. I wanna believe that.

DELLA. I'm telling you, Poppa.

JESSE. It didn't show. You come in here every night for six months and everything that passed between us was a lie.

DELLA. But not everything I felt.

JESSE. That takes some buying.

DELLA. But it fits. You and me, Pop, always been a hard road. Like tonight. You only played to hit back at me.

JESSE. I played because I found some hurt that I couldn't shift no other way. I sang those blues tonight like no one sings 'em any more. Those boys. They're smart. And they're quick. But they ain't the real thing. What those kids saw tonight was the last performance of the real thing. I'd forgot how good I was. No one'll forget now.

DELLA. No one's ever gonna forget you.

JESSE. Where you gonna go?

DELLA. Karl says he can get me away.

JESSE. Karl?

DELLA. Some place Mexico.

JESSE. Yeah?

DELLA. But what do I do after that?

He goes to the black attaché case. He gives it to her.

DELLA. That's your money, Pop.

JESSE. I don't need it.

DELLA. Keep it for yourself.

JESSE. I don't need it.

DELLA *places the attaché case by the travelling bag.*

DELLA. Thanks, Pop.

KARL *appears on the porch.*

KARL. It's a lot quieter out there.

JESSE. Sounds a whole lot quieter.

KARL. Old people move surprisingly fast when you drive a Cadillac at them.

Pause.

My chauffeur is phoning the helicopter right now. You want to take that trip?

Pause.

DELLA. O.K.

KARL *goes onto the porch and signals to the chauffeur.*
JESSE *stands. He goes to* DELLA *and embraces her.*

JESSE. When you're on the run, you got to vary your pace.
Fast, then slow. Fast, then slow.

DELLA. Yeah?

JESSE. That's the key.

JESSE *sits again. His back to* DELLA. *Outside, the
Cadillac hoots.* DELLA *picks up the travelling bag and the
attaché case and leaves. Some moments.* KARL *waves at
the chauffeur. The Cadillac pulls away.* KARL *comes back
in.*

KARL. Jesse, I feel bad about what's happened. Della, the
church. I done some bad things to your life here.

JESSE. Can't say I liked my life that much.

KARL. Right.

JESSE. But, it was a life, know what I'm saying.

KARL. Man, you don't have to stay here. You can come with
me in the Cadillac. Hole up with the band. I can set you up.
Money. Gigs. Deals. You're going to be one hot property.

JESSE. Lose one life, get another.

KARL. That's what I'm saying.

JESSE. Whole new life.

KARL. The things we talked about. The album, the tour.
They're yours. I can give you any life you want.

Pause.

JESSE. Karl, you wanna know the truth 'bout that cross roads
shit?

KARL. You said it wasn't true.

JESSE. It's true. Question is, you wanna hear it?

KARL. Yeah. I wanna hear it.

Pause.

JESSE. I was twenty years old. I bought myself a cheap guitar, carried it about with me every place. I would take it down the Saturday night frolics, wait for the main act to break and get up on that stage. But I just weren't no good. Couldn't play a lick. I had people crazy to take that thing off of me. Then one day I hear that old witch doctor story and it worked on me. A voice in the ear, whisperin' at me all the time: 'Go to them cross roads. What you got to lose? Ain't frighted of that Devil stuff is you, boy?' One Saturday evening, I head off, alone, on the road with the guitar, don't know to where. Hungry, thirsty, walkin' in the dark, goin' north, places I'd never been, walked all night, walked all next day and into Sunday night. I don't know how far I walked, sixty, seventy, mile. Passed dozens of crossroads. Got dark again, pitch dark. Couldn't see where I was headin'. Then I find myself at a place with two roads meeting, hell, not even roads, more kind of a couple of tracks, mule tracks at best. And there was a wooden crate there. I felt tired, sat down. I figured it for midnight, I didn't know. But I started to play and sing. My fingers felt, you know how they do sometimes, clumsy, couldn't get no juice out of them, and my voice kinda ragged. Sat there and sang 'One Dime Blues'. Even I knew it weren't no good but I got through it and then I heard something. Footsteps in the dark. I just sits there tight and the footsteps stop right behind me. I don't turn around or nothin'. And this hand reaches forward, grabs the guitar and tunes it right down, open D tuning, some crazy thing I never heard before. Hands it back, starts to walk away and I say. 'Who the hell are you?' And he don't say nothin'. But he just turns his head, not even half a turn, a little quarter turn and I see a flash of that face in the moonlight. I saw it man. Don't tell me I didn't see it.

KARL. What you see?

JESSE. The face was white. I saw the Devil's face and he was white.

Pause.

KARL. What are you saying? (*Pause.*) That's not what happened.

JESSE. No? Was you there, Karl?

KARL. That's not what happened then.

JESSE. Well now.

Pause.

KARL. Are you making a statement here?

Pause.

Jesse?

The Cadillac pulls up and hoots.

Any deal you want is yours. What you gonna do, just sit it out in this shack till you go to your grave?

JESSE. You know, Karl. I had me a fine time today and I don't have no regrets. But your Cadillac is there and you'd best be on that road.

KARL. Man. I need you.

JESSE. How does a blues man travel, Karl?

KARL. I don't wanna hear it.

JESSE. How does a blues man travel?

KARL. Down the road. Guitar in his hand.

Pause.

JESSE. Yeah?

KARL. Down the road. Guitar in his hand. Alone.

JESSE. That's the riff.

KARL. I can't do it, Jesse.

JESSE. Alone. That's the part that cuts.

KARL. Yeah.

JESSE. You see the road?

KARL. I see it.

JESSE. You see the guitar?

KARL. *This* guitar?

JESSE. Angela.

Pause.

KARL. I can't take her, man.

JESSE. I can't come with you. Take her.

Pause. KARL *picks up the guitar case.*

KARL. I got her, Jesse.

JESSE. Well now. Cadillac makes the road easy. Guitar make the blues come easy. The other thing is hard. So long, Karl.

KARL. You're just down after the high. I'll come back tomorrow.

Pause.

Feelings run high. I'll come back when it's cool.

Pause.

Jesse, man. I'm sorry if things went wrong for you.

Pause.

So long. Was a privilege.

JESSE. Yeah.

KARL *goes. Some moments.* JESSE *stands, goes to the porch, looks out. Walks back in. Picks up the hat, plays with it. The Cadillac pulls away. In the distance, the sound of a helicopter.* JESSE *sits, pours a drink, gulps it down. He pulls himself together as if for a great effort. He leans forward in his chair. He takes several deep breaths. He sings.*

JESSE. He rose, he rose –

The hymn catches in his throat. He makes another effort.

He rose from the dead –

JESSE *struggles to get the words out. He drinks again.*

And my Lord –

The words stick again. JESSE*'s mouth is open, but no sound emerges, as if he were retching silently. He stops, takes another drink. He sits back in his chair. He puts the hat on his head and closes his eyes. Then, effortlessly he begins to sing the blues.*

You may bury my body down by the highway side
You may bury my body down by the highway side
So my old evil spirit can catch a greyhound bus and ride.

The lights fade slowly to

Blackout.

End.

A Nick Hern Book

I Just Stopped by to See the Man first published in Great
Britain in 2000 as a paperback original by Nick Hern Books,
14 Larden Road, London W3 7ST in association with
the Royal Court Theatre, London

Typeset by Country Setting, Kingsdown, Kent, CT14 8ES
Printed and bound in Great Britain by Biddles of Guildford

ISBN 1 85459 482 6

A CIP catalogue record for this book is available from
the British Library